New York State Canals

A Short History

WEIGHMASTER'S OFFIC

New York State CANALS

A SHORT HISTORY

by F. Daniel Larkin

PURPLE MOUNTAIN PRESS
Fleischmanns, New York

Dedication

For Kendall Larkin Gillette.
May she and all New Yorkers enjoy the heritage of the State's canals.

New York State Canals: A Short History
First Edition 1998

Published by
PURPLE MOUNTAIN PRESS, LTD.
Main Street, P.O. Box 309
Fleischmanns, New York 12430-0309
845-254-4062, 845-254-4476 (fax)
purple@catskill.net

Library of Congress Cataloging-in-Publication Data

Larkin, F. Daniel, 1938-
New York State canals : a short history / F. Daniel Larkin.
p. cm.
Includes bibliographical references (p.) and index.
ISBN 0-935796-90-8 (pbk : alk. paper)
1. Canals- -New York (State)- -History. I. Title.
TC624.N7L37 1997
386'.46'09747- -dc21 97-40532
CIP

Manufactured in the United States of America on acid-free paper.

Cover and Frontispiece:
"The Albany Basin or Canal Harbor of the Erie and Champlain Canals,"
from *Frank Leslie's Illustrated Newspaper*, Vol. 2, No. 50, November 22, 1856.

10 9 8 7 6 5 4

Table of Contents

Introduction

NEW YORK'S ERIE CANAL has long been heralded in story and song and the legendary waterway is well known to many people throughout the world. Far fewer, though, are aware of the vast, 524-mile canal network that still exists in the state.

Although canals in New York first appeared in the eighteenth century, it was the building of the Erie Canal during the first quarter of the nineteenth century that launched New York State and the nation into the canal era; arguably, no other enterprise was as responsible for creating the "Empire State" as was the Erie. There is no question that the Erie Canal was an economic success. In addition to the business it brought the state, more than $120 million in tolls were collected on it during the nineteenth century, paying for its original cost and the first enlargement, as well as maintenance. But many of the state's other canals did not share the Erie's triumph, and the story of New York's canals is one of contrast between those that contributed to the growth and development of the state and those that did not.

An appendix to the 1905 *Annual Report of the New York State Engineer and Surveyor*, submitted to the legislature in 1906, remains the most complete history of New York's canals. Its two volumes, entitled *History of the Canal System* *ot the State of New York*, written by Noble E. Whitford, encompass 1,547 pages of detailed information about the system as it then existed. Much of the literature that has appeared since centers on the Erie Canal in the nineteenth century; relatively little has been written about New York's other canals, many of which connected with the Erie. Except for Whitford's *History of the Barge Canal of New York State* (1922), largely dealing with construction, during the past 80 years, the Barge Canal System has gone practically unnoticed—only recently some reminiscences have begun to appear.* In regard to the connecting canals, much of what has been done are guides prepared in conjunction with canal field trips sponsored by the Canal Society of New York State.

This short history is not meant to be as definitive as the Whitford volumes, but to acquaint the reader with New York's canals, including the changes that occurred in the twentieth century. It is intended to fill the information gap until a more detailed account of New York's canals is written.

*Michele McFee has written the first comprehensive history of the Barge Canal: *The Long Haul* (Fleischmanns, NY: Purple Mountain Press, 1998).

I. Improving Upon Nature

A TRAVELER along the Hudson or Mohawk Rivers cannot help but notice that both waterways scoured deep channels through the rugged terrain bordering their banks. This natural excavation resulted in the only water-level route through the Appalachians, the mountain barrier separating the eastern coastal region from the interior. The Hudson, rising in the Adirondack Mountains, flows some 300 miles south to the Atlantic Ocean. For half its distance—from New York's capital region to New York harbor—it is a fjord-like river that can easily accommodate ocean vessels. Albany has a port facility today, as it has had for 380 years. Ten miles north of Albany, the Mohawk joins the Hudson. In its 150-mile journey from the southerly part of the Tug Hill Plateau, the Mohawk carves a 100-mile-long west-to-east valley through New York's Appalachian uplands. As a result, it provides a major portion of a water-level connection between the Hudson and the Great Lakes. From where the Mohawk turns east at Rome, it is possible to complete the water path westward to Lake Ontario via Wood Creek, Oneida Lake, the Oneida River, and the Oswego River.

The Hudson-Mohawk water-level course through the Appalachians is a topographic asset that greatly contributed to New York's growth and development. It, coupled with the superior harbor at New York City and the Lake Ontario link to the other Great Lakes, was nature's chief contribution to the creation of the Empire State.

People have used New York's water routes to the interior for centuries. With the arrival of Europeans early in the seventeenth century and the resulting increase in trade between the newcomers and Native Americans, utilization of the water-level route increased. European colonization of New York commenced with New Netherlands, a Dutch enterprise that hugged the Hudson River and its environs. Although Fort Orange (Albany) was built as a trading post in 1624, it was 1660 before the Dutch ventured west to found Schenectady on the Mohawk River, only 16 miles from Fort Orange. The colony's chief reason for existence was the fur trade, carried on mainly through the Mohawk Valley, with goods exchanged at Fort Orange, then shipped down the Hudson to New Amsterdam or directly to the Netherlands.

In 1664, the Dutch lost their foothold in North America to the English, who promptly changed the name of the colony to New York, in honor of its new proprietor, the Duke of York, and Anglicized many of the place names as well. New Amsterdam became New York, and Fort Orange became Albany. Soon expansion occurred, especially into the Mohawk Valley.

By the close of the seventeenth century, the importance of the route underscored the need for its improvement. In 1700, colonial Secretary for Indian Affairs Robert Livingston wrote to the Earl of Bellomont, the colony's governor, about the Little Carrying Place (Little Falls) "and the Great Carrying Place [Rome]. . .reckoned 12 miles; with some change could be shortened to 4, there being a creek [Wood Creek] which leads to the Oneyde River, now full of wood, which may easily be cleared and a small dam be made, which being let open will furnish water for canoes or batoes in the dryest time of summer."[1]

At this time, the powerful Five Nations of the Iroquois dominated New York between the Hudson and the Great Lakes, and they controlled trade between the native inhabitants of the lakes and the Europeans. The importance of this trade is evident from a plea made in July 1702 by an Iroquois leader Tehonwahonkarachqua to Governor Cornbury that the "path over ye [Great] Carrying Place may be mark'd upon ye trees and ye old trees be taken out of ye Creek which much injures the Passage of Canoes."[2] Cornbury ordered the path marked and the creek cleared "for ye ease and accommodation of all strangers."[3] During the summer of 1725, some 57 canoes from Albany crossed the Great Carrying Place and returned with 738 packs of beaver and deer skins.[4] Within the next two decades, the British built forts to protect the western part of the route at what are now Rome and Oswego.

The eighteenth-century struggle for empire between the British and the French led to three wars in North America between 1702 and 1763. Because of its long border with New France in the north, the English colony of New York was involved in all three, especially the French and Indian War of the 1750s and early 1760s, when the Hudson-Mohawk corridor became increasingly important for the movement of troops and supplies to northern and western New York, where most of the fighting took place. By then, settlement extended north of Albany to Lake George and Lake Champlain, and west along the Mohawk.

Bateaux, or battoes, gradually replaced canoes as the river craft of choice, since they were built stronger and could carry a greater load. The Swedish naturalist Peter Kalm, traveling near Albany in 1749, described bateaux as shallow-draft craft made of white pine boards 18 to 24 feet long, about 40 inches wide, pointed at both ends, with nearly perpendicular sides 20 to 24 inches high. They were rowed and carried a load of one-and-a-half tons.[5] Later, bateaux were built longer and wider to boost their capacity as trade increased along the Mohawk.

By the outbreak of the American Revolution in 1775, settlement in central New York extended to the small community of Deerfield (across the Mohawk from where Utica is today) with three or four families living 15 miles upstream near Fort Stanwix on the Great Carry. Settlers at the Carry made their living moving goods on wagons across the flat stretch between the Mohawk River and Wood Creek. Once fighting started, the people at Fort Stanwix and Deerfield scurried eastward into the middle valley for better protection against marauding Royalist forces. By 1784, the year after the peace treaty, settlers began returning to the western Mohawk Valley and beyond. An isolated settlement consisting mostly of New Englanders grew at Canandaigua, 100 miles west of Fort Stanwix. The newcomers were the vanguard of a mass migration from New England known as the "Yankee Invasion." For the next four decades, thousands of "Yankees" seeking cheap, fertile land poured into central, western, and northern New York. Many pushed even farther west into the region called "The Ohio." This sudden population spurt put increased demands on a trade system ill prepared to handle the new commerce. Improvements were necessary.

Although changes in the watercourse between the Hudson River and the Great Lakes had been sought since the end of the seventeenth century, it was not until 1792 that a joint stock venture, the Western Inland Lock Navigation Company, was organized under the leadership of General Philip Schuyler for the specific purpose of improving the route. A second firm, the Northern Inland Lock Navigation Company, sought to improve the route between the northern Hudson River and Lake Champlain, though it failed with little accomplished.

The Western Inland Lock Navigation Company soon found that natural impediments to navigation were not the only obstacles to its success. Even with the backing of powerful land speculators with immense holdings in western New York, and with the support of prominent bankers, the company found raising sufficient funds an ongoing problem. The state legislature responded in the second half of the 1790s with both contributions and loans to help keep the company solvent.

A Durham boat "navigating on the Mohawk River" at a wing dam of the Western Inland Lock Navigation Company, 1810. In the foreground is a bateau.

Courtesy of the Canal Society of New York State

The company commenced in 1793 to clear the Wood Creek channel and to straighten the sharpest bends, which effectively shortened the creek by seven miles. Next, a canal with five wooden lift locks was cut through the rock at Little Falls to circumvent the falls in the Mohawk River.

Initially, the lack of trained engineers proved a serious problem. Schuyler therefore personally supervised the work, but his obvious lack of engineering knowledge led to renewed attempts to secure an experienced builder. Eventually, the part-time services of William Weston, an English engineer working on a Pennsylvania canal, helped to improve the situation. Labor supply also presented a problem, and the search for men extended to the surrounding states as well as Canada. An attempt was made to hire Native Americans, but this quickly failed; some of them briefly threatened workers on the Wood Creek improvement.

Lock construction included much experimentation with wood, brick, and stone. Adequate mortar was not found until 1803, and many locks needed to be rebuilt several times.[6] By 1797, a canal nearly two miles long was dug across the Great Carry at Fort Stanwix, and soon additional shorter canals were constructed to bypass some dangerous rapids in the Mohawk River. During the first decade of the nineteenth century, Benjamin Wright (the future chief engineer of the Erie Canal) directed the emplacement of four locks on Wood Creek for improved navigation. The company also extended improvements to the Seneca River in order to tap commerce from the area adjoining the two largest Finger Lakes, Seneca and Cayuga.

Eliminating the carries, straightening the stream and bypassing major rapids paved the way for the use of larger craft, called Durham or Schenectady boats. Fifty to 60 feet long by 8 feet broad and equipped with a sail in addition to the boatmen who moved the vessel with heavy wooden poles, Durham boats had eight times the cargo capacity of bateaux. The sail mast was hinged near its base so it could be lowered to allow the boat to pass under bridges. Use of these bigger boats reduced the cost of freight shipment between Albany and Seneca Lake from $100 to $32 a ton, and lowered transportation costs from Albany to the Niagara frontier by 50 percent.[7]

The Western Inland Lock Navigation Company's works between the Hudson River, Lake Ontario, and the Finger Lakes region was a series of waterway improvements, not a single canal. Although the constructions allowed larger craft to use the natural waterway, they did not eliminate nature's control. Floods, low water resulting from dry spells, and the fact that boats on the 100-mile stretch from Schenectady to Fort Stanwix (Rome) had to move upstream against the powerful current of the Mohawk all hindered transportation on the river. In addition, population growth along the Schenectady-to-Niagara frontier axis rapidly expanded from roughly 95,000 people in 1800 to more than 226,000 by 1810, challenging the limitations of the water transportation system. The movement of troops and war material to New York's western and northern frontiers during the War of 1812 made especially heavy demands upon the inadequate water route.

When horses pulled boats:
Changing teams on a loaded boat on the Erie Canal at Durhamville, looking southeast, 1905.

Courtesy of the Canal Society of New York State

II. The Erie Canal

THE DRIVE FOR IMPROVEMENTS in the state's water transportation system started even before the War of 1812. Early in 1808, Assemblyman Joshua Forman, a Federalist from Onondaga County, introduced a resolution in the state legislature to survey a canal route between the Hudson River and Lake Erie. The motion was seconded by another Federalist, Benjamin Wright of Oneida County. Wright had some experience with waterways, since he earlier had surveyed more than 100 miles of the region north of the Finger Lakes for the Western Inland Lock Navigation Company. James Geddes, chosen to run the survey in 1808, reported on two possible routes: one included Lake Ontario from Oswego to the Niagara River, with a canal along the river to Lake Erie; the other was an interior canal directly to Lake Erie.

Another route examination was authorized in 1810, this time overseen by a canal board of seven commissioners. The following year the legislature passed the state's first canal law. The original commissioners were reappointed and two more were added, including the state's "expert" on steamboat navigation, Robert Fulton. The commissioners' assignment included seeking national aid for canal construction, finding other sources for financial support, obtaining land grants along the projected canal route, and negotiating for the purchase of the short canals and other improvements belonging to the Western Inland Lock Navigation Company.[8] DeWitt Clinton, a leading Democratic-Republican, former mayor of New York City and nephew of long-time New York governor George Clinton, was the most active among the commissioners to push for canal plans.

The transportation problems that arose during the War of 1812 gave additional impetus to constructing a canal across New York, so as soon as peace returned, canal advocates renewed their efforts. But by 1816 it was obvious that the hoped-for national financial aid would not be forthcoming. As a result, DeWitt Clinton spearheaded a drive to bombard the state legislature with petitions in favor of a state-funded project. Final success came in the 1817 legislative session, when an act was passed authorizing construction of a canal from the Hudson River to Lake Erie. The route was divided into three sections and an engineer designated to head each section. The portion from the Hudson to Rome was to be under the supervision of Charles Broadhead, the section from Rome to the Seneca River would be supervised by Benjamin Wright, and the section from the Seneca River to Lake Erie would be under the direction of James Geddes.

Building a canal from Albany to Lake Erie meant digging a ditch 363 miles long, 40 feet wide at the surface of the water, 28 feet wide at the bottom, and 4 feet deep. Since Lake Erie is nearly 565 feet higher than the Hudson at Albany, it also required 83 locks, each 90 feet by 15 feet. In 1817, nearly all excavation and construction was done by pick-and-shovel labor and animal power. Since dynamite was not yet invented, black gunpowder (with relatively lower explosive pressure) was used for blasting, and all drilling to set the powder was done by hand.

Some historians have said that among the few machines used were two ingenious ones developed to topple trees and pull stumps. Even the largest trees could be felled by a device that worked with a line attached near the tree top and wound on a wheel fastened to an endless screw. The stump-pulling machine consisted of an axle 30 feet long and 20 inches in diameter resting on wheels with a diameter of 16 feet. A third wheel 14 feet in diameter was attached at the midpoint of the axle. The apparatus was placed over the stump to be pulled and the stump was attached to chains wound around the axle. Draft animals then pulled a rope wound around the center wheel and the stump was lifted and hauled away.[9]

The much-anticipated ceremony to begin construction occurred on July 4, 1817, when dignitaries gathered near the United States Arsenal in Rome to witness the event. There, in the marshy lowland between the Mohawk River and Wood Creek, Canal Commissioner Samuel Young accurately predicted that via the Erie Canal, "unborn millions will easily transport their surplus productions to the shores of the Atlantic, procure their supplies, and hold a useful and profitable intercourse with all the maritime nations of the earth," after which Judge John Richardson, holder of the initial contract, overturned the first spadeful of earth.[10] It was the start of a new era.

Building the Erie Canal was an immense undertaking for the little more than one million people of New York State. Even if the cost had been limited to the $4 million estimate, it would have been a huge outlay for the time—but the final figure was nearly double the initial calculation. With nearly 3,000 men and a quarter as many draft animals toiling away on the middle section alone, 94 miles of ditch from Utica to Montezuma were opened by 1820, and work was under way on both the eastern and western sections. The newly completed section was put to immediate use and the tolls collected helped to pay for it and the unfinished portions.

Even in the face of seemingly instant success, there was considerable opposition to the Erie Canal. The bulk of the state's population resided along the Hudson River corridor from New York City to Albany, and many of the citizens there could not understand the urgency of spending state dollars to extend a canal to Lake Erie at a time when western New York for the most part still was sparsely settled frontier. Of course, the residents of the Hudson Valley could access a superb natural water highway—the Hudson River—free of charge, which may partly explain their lack of enthusiasm. While the financial success of the completed portions of the canal helped to blunt opposition, the reelection of DeWitt Clinton as governor in 1820 also did much to assure the continuation of the project.

A major problem in constructing the stone structures on the canal was locating a source for *hydraulic cement* that would harden under water. Both locks and waste weirs (structures designed to eliminate excess water and keep a constant four-foot water depth) required the use of cement to hold the stone in place. Since a portion of the structures always was submerged, hydraulic cement was required, even though at first the contractors felt that common quick lime would suffice. Wright warned the commissioners that quick lime would not do and advised them to import hydraulic cement from Europe, since there was no known domestic source. Soon after Wright's recommendation, canal engineer Canvass White discovered limestone near Chittenango that, when burned, pulverized, and mixed with sand, produced a cement that hardened under water. White is thus credited with discovering America's first hydraulic cement.[11]

Other challenges included swamps to be crossed, valleys to be spanned, and ridges to be excavated. In the vast Cayuga marshes (Montezuma Swamp), diggers were forced to work in up to a foot of water. Fever struck down so many workers in the summers of 1820 and 1821 that scores of immigrant Irish were brought from New York City as replacements. Contractors found it necessary to pay them as much as $1.25

per day to coerce them to brave the pestilence, but by spring 1822 the miasmal mire had been crossed. The higher pay probably helped some of the Irish workers to achieve the dreams that had brought them to the United States initially. In 1834, an Irish immigrant farmer who had been a canal laborer spoke of his "fine farm of land now, which I own outright"—the canal had allowed him to return to his traditional agrarianism.[12]

Farther west, near Rochester, contractors encountered the Irondequoit Creek valley. A quarter-mile-long earth embankment was created to support the canal 70 feet above the creek bottom. The next significant obstacle was the Genesee River, which rises near the New York-Pennsylvania border and flows north to enter Lake Ontario at Rochester. An 802-foot-long masonry aqueduct carried the canal over the Genesee at that burgeoning mill town.[13]

Next came the seemingly impossible task of taking the canal over the Niagara escarpment, a job so daunting that the canal commissioners themselves took control and used state resources to hire a thousand men to cut a 7-mile-long, 127-foot-wide channel up to 30 feet deep. Two miles of it were blasted and scraped out of solid limestone. At the eastern end of the trench, five sets of locks were needed to overcome nearly 70 feet difference in elevation. The construction camp that sprouted around the locks soon evolved into a village called Lockport.[14]

While laborers dug the canal toward Lake Erie, work continued on the eastern section. From Utica to Schenectady, the canal followed the south bank of the Mohawk River. At Little Falls, a feeder canal 1,184 feet long, including a stone aqueduct, was built across the Mohawk to provide water for the canal. It also served as a waterway to the village on the north side of the river. East of Schenectady, the canal followed the Mohawk's north bank, then re-crossed to the south side before its union with the Hudson River at Albany. Two stone aqueducts (one of which, at 1,137, feet was the longest on the entire canal) and 27 locks connected Schenectady and Albany.[15]

Finally, at the end of October 1825, the Erie Canal was completed and ready for the much-anticipated opening celebration. At 10 A.M. on October 26, a flotilla of boats entered the canal at Buffalo for the 500-mile journey to New York City. Led by the *Seneca Chief*, which carried Governor DeWitt Clinton and other dignitaries, the small fleet also included *Noah's Ark*, with a cargo of products from the West (including a bear and two eagles). Ninety minutes later the signal of the procession's start was received in New York City---ingeniously accomplished by a relay of cannon fire

Entrance to the Erie Canal from the Hudson River at Albany.
From *Frank Leslie's Illustrated Newspaper*, Vol. 2, No. 50, November 22, 1856

along the banks of the canal and the Hudson River. The steady movement of boats through the artificial waterway was interrupted only by obligatory stops at communities along the route to properly mark the occasion. Joshua Forman, the legislator who introduced the first Erie Canal resolution in 1808, delivered an address at Syracuse. At Albany, civilian and military officials attended a ceremony at the State Capitol; afterward, 600 guests dined at tables placed upon a gaily decorated bridge across the canal basin.[16]

The canal boats left Albany towed by steamboats and arrived in New York Harbor a day later, on November 4. The festivities there eclipsed all others. In a naval ceremony off Sandy Hook, Governor Clinton poured a keg of Lake Erie water into the Atlantic to symbolize the "wedding of the waters." The day's activities were brought to a close with the simultaneous illumination of many homes and buildings, and a huge display of fireworks. City Hall alone sparkled with the light of 2,300 lamps and candles. A grand canal ball on November 7 was the finale; the center of attraction was a miniature canal boat made of New York maple sugar floating in a large container of Lake Erie water. Gold medals struck in honor of the event were sent to several prominent people, including President John Quincy Adams, former presidents, and the Marquis de Lafayette, the last surviving major-general of the patriot army of the Revolution. Upon receiving his medal, Thomas Jefferson replied on June 8, 1826, less than a month before his death, that the Erie Canal would bestow "wealth and prosperity" upon the people of New York. New Yorkers, had "built the longest canal in the world in the least time, with the least experience, for the least money, and to the greatest public benefit."[17]

In Walter D. Edmonds' *Rome Haul*, his classic novel depicting canal life, an itinerant peddler describes the Erie Canal as "a swarming hive. Boats coming and going. . .freight going west and raw food east. . .people going west. . .people coming east. But the canawlers keep a-moving. By grab, it's the bowels of the nation! It's the whole shebang of life."[18] His words accurately and succinctly captured the essence of what the canal was all about.

Commerce commenced on the canal as soon as each section was opened. The Erie Canal Navigation Company of Rome started the packet (passenger-boat) business when it put the *Chief Engineer* and the *Montezuma* into service in 1820. Even though the cost was at least $1,500 each for the approximately 80-foot by 14-foot boats, company profits were considerable. Soon competition challenged the company's monopoly and business thrived, particularly after the entire length of the canal was opened. Packets carried between 50 and 100 passengers, had six or seven crew members, and were pulled by teams of horses or mules.[19] The companies that operated packet boats usually kept their draft animals in barns along the canal. This made it easy to change teams in order to keep the three- to four-miles-per-hour pace, as advertised. Freight boats were generally family owned and contained living quarters and a stable in addition to the cargo hold.

Travel on the Erie Canal was described by both Americans and Europeans. Among narrations by Americans was that of Sybil Tatum, a teenager who left an account of her family's 1830 journey from New Jersey to Ohio via the canal. She seemed satisfied with her experience, as did Anne Royall and Thomas Woodcock, other contemporary travelers who were pleased with their accommodations. Writer Nathaniel Hawthorne, however, was less enamored with it. He found passage along the Rome summit level so uninteresting that he departed the boat for a walk through the fields and was nearly left behind.

Europeans who experienced the Erie Canal usually were less than complimentary, especially with the sleeping accommodations. Narrow beds or bunks were suspended from the walls or sides of the packets by cords, which would allow

"Travelling on the Erie Canal" at the Noses in the Mohawk Valley near Sprakers, 1825.

Courtesy of the Canal Society of New York State

"Entrance to the Harbor, Lockport," from Colden's *Memoir* (1825)

Courtesy of the New York State Library

them to be folded against the walls during the day.) A Swede traveling in the mid-1830s objected to the sleeping arrangements, and described the chaos that followed when, due to a hard scrape from another boat, bunk cords snapped and "about a dozen sleeping individuals were precipitated from the second and third tier [of bunks] on the unfortunate beings who were lying on the floor."[20] A Scottish traveler in 1843 was more detailed regarding the beds---he likened them to "shelves about eighteen inches apart" which accommodated the men in the "after part of the cabin," as well as the women who were "stowed away" forward behind a temporary screen. After commenting on the "stench and effluvia from such a collection of living beings," he complained that "breakfast was laid out in the same apartment, without any attempt at ventillation [*sic*]." He warned his countrymen against "travelling much by canal in the States."[21]

Harriet Martineau, an Englishwoman in America in 1838, was even more negative. "I would never advise ladies to travel by canal" in New York unless the boats were "far better kept than any that I saw or heard of on" the Erie Canal. She complained about sitting on the deck above the cabin and "having to duck under bridges every quarter of an hour, under penalty of having one's head crushed to atoms," and lamented about the "heat and noise, the known vicinity of a compressed crowd, lying packed like herrings in a barrel."[22]

Both Europeans and Americans increasingly used the canal as the gateway to the West and as a cheaper and more comfortable means of accessing New York's sparsely settled interior than overland transportation. As an "artificial river [the Erie Canal] provided inexpensive transportation for passengers whose journeys could not have been anticipated by its sponsors."[23] Examples of unanticipated journeys included those of runaway slaves who were spirited along the canal from Syracuse to Buffalo and then to freedom across the Canadian border.[24] The canal thus insured that New

York, which in 1820 had surpassed Virginia as the nation's most populous state, would remain so, for population growth in villages along the Erie's route was phenomenal. As early as 1825, 42 boats carrying roughly a thousand passengers passed through Utica each day.[25] During the 1820s, Albany experienced a 96 percent population growth, Utica 183 percent, Syracuse 282 percent, Buffalo 314 percent, and Rochester increased a whopping 512 percent.[26] The amazing surge of people continued unabated after the entire canal was opened. Between 1825 and 1835, Albany, Troy, Utica, Syracuse, and Lockport all doubled in population, while Rochester nearly tripled and Buffalo almost quadrupled. Of the larger communities along the canal, only Schenectady and Rome failed to keep pace. The expansion of each was held to between 25 and 30 percent.[27] The reasons for Schenectady's lag are somewhat unclear, but undoubtedly Rome's modest growth compared to other canal villages stemmed from its location about a mile north of the Erie Canal—its connection to the main line of the canal was via the narrower, short canal built by the Western Inland Lock Navigation Company during the 1790s.

Of course, the Erie Canal carried freight as well as people, and its completion drove down shipping costs. Before the Erie opened, wheat from the Genesee Valley worth 62.5¢ a bushel, cost $2.15 in Albany—it took 20 days to make the 230-mile trip by an ox-pulled wagon. With the opening of the canal, the cost of moving a ton of wheat fell from $100 to $5, and it took only ten days to make the trip from Buffalo all the way to New York City.[28] In 1825, eastbound cargoes on

Facing Page:

"Beauty on the Barge Deck," from *The National Police Gazette*, July 22, 1882.

Courtesy of the Canal Society of New York State

the canal totaled 185,000 tons, including 562,000 bushels of wheat, 221,000 barrels of flour, 435,000 gallons of spirits, and 32 million board feet of lumber. Westbound goods totaled 32,000 tons of mostly domestic and imported manufactures.[29] Soon, though, westbound tonnage surpassed eastbound freight: In 1840, 158,148 tons of goods came from the west, but 309,167 tons went west.[30] Total value of all freight was $73 million.[31]

Twenty years later, the tonnage shipped on the canal again tipped in favor of western produce. In 1860, 1,896,975 tons of items went east, while only 379,086 tons of goods traveled west.[32] This was due in part to the emerging "product specialization" occurring in canal communities. Rochester, for example, specialized in flour, Utica in cloth, and Syracuse in salt.[33] The burgeoning trade from the West also had a depressing impact on eastern farming; one agricultural historian traced the abandonment of farms in New England to the Erie Canal's opening.[34]

"Empire Dry Dock and Residence of W. J. Wheeler" on the Erie Canal near Cohoes, c. 1870.

Courtesy of the Canal Society of New York State

Another result of the expansion of commerce on the canal was the immense revenue it generated for the state. When the Erie's first section opened, tolls collected in 1820 on it and the short canals of the Western Inland Lock Navigation Company amounted to a modest $28,000; four years later 10,000 boats laden with cargo paid $300,000 in tolls.[35] By 1834, there were 16,834 freight- and packet-boat clearances at Albany alone,[36] or the equivalent of 70 boats per day.

If building the Erie Canal opened the way for the development of the Albany-to-Buffalo corridor, it had a similar effect on New York City. In 1818, the city's hinterland (the inland region that trades through it) consisted of much of New York State, eastern New Jersey, and western Connecticut; its population of 1,170,000 people was an impressive one-sixth of the national total and contributed to the city's importance as a leading port. But the opening of the Erie Canal clinched New York's position as America's premier

"Tow winding through the Highlands, West Point" on the Hudson River by Augusta Brown, 1896.

Courtesy of the New York State Museum

A.J. DEAN
JERSEY CITY

port.[37] By 1827, western flour trade alone via the Erie Canal to New York City totaled 625,000 barrels, nearly two-and-a-half times the 1820 amount---New York City commanded first place in the flour trade, ahead of second-place Baltimore and third-place Philadelphia.[38] The commerce in flour demonstrates only part of the Erie Canal's impact on New York City. There is little doubt that the "Erie Canal played its part in adding the West [to the City's hinterland], and the financial bonds which resulted were so strong that the subsequent efforts of the rival ports to tap that region with railroads did not shake the pre-dominance of New York."[39]

Soon after the completion of the Erie, it became apparent that the canal wasn't large enough to handle the increasing traffic. Former chief engineer Benjamin Wright realized this, and in 1834 admitted to Canal Commissioner William C. Bouck that "we see in the size of our Canal that we have made great errors, very great indeed" and cautioned the commissioners not to repeat past mistakes.[40] The following year, the state legislature approved an enlargement to 70 feet wide and 7 feet deep. Most of the locks would be doubled to allow for traffic to pass both ways simultaneously, and all would be increased in size to 110 feet by 18 feet. Since lock dimensions governed the size of the boats, boatyards responded by launching craft with 210- to 240-ton capacity, more than triple the capacity of the first canal boats on the Erie. Con-

Facing Page, Above:

"Grain-Elevator Transferring Cargo from a Canal-Boat to a Ship," New York City, from *Harper's Weekly*, November 15, 1873

Facing Page, Bellow:

"Canal Boats in Winter Quarters" on the New Jersey shore, from *Leslie's Illustrated*, May 6, 1871.

Both courtesy of the Canal Society of New York State

struction on the enlarged canal commenced in 1836. Minor route changes reduced the length of the Erie from 363 to 350.5 miles and the number of lift locks declined from 83 to 72.[41]

While construction continued on the Erie enlargement, so did the movement of goods and people. In 1845, tonnage topped one million for the first time. Although it took 20 years of growth for Erie tonnage to exceed a million tons per year, the two-million mark was broken only seven years later, and only a decade later, in 1862, with Civil War shipping making new demands on the canal's capacity, more than three million tons were carried on New York's artificial waterway. Although more than three million tons of shipping passed through the canal each year over much of the next three decades, it wasn't until 1880 that the four-million-ton total was reached: The 4,608,651 tons shipped that year was the most carried in any single year of the Erie Canal's history.[42]

As shipping on the Erie Canal sharply increased, so did the population of the canal's principal communities. Between 1835 and 1850, Albany, Troy, and Lockport nearly doubled in size; Rome's growth rate was close behind, since the

Facing Page, Above:

Brizolara's Canal Grocery at Erie Canal Lock 44 in Frankfort, from *History of Herkimer County*, 1879

Facing Page, Below:

J. F. Brown's lumber and coal yard and grocery store, from *History of Montgomery and Fulton Counties*, 1878.

Both courtesy of the Canal Society of New York State

J.C. BRIZOLARA.
ICE
OATS & HAY

J.F. BROWNS
GROCERY STORE
J. F. BROWNS LUMBER YARD
COAL
COAL
WAMBA

enlargement brought the canal directly through the village. The population of Rochester and Buffalo more than doubled and the size of Syracuse tripled. Only Utica and Schenectady lagged behind the others in rapid growth, with the former community growing by about 70 percent and the latter by approximately one-third. Albany, with 50,753 people in 1850, remained the largest of the canal's cities and villages.[43]

But by 1850, another method of transportation had appeared in New York State which also contributed to the population explosion between Albany and Buffalo. In December 1825—two months after the completion of the Erie Canal—an advertisement in a Schenectady newspaper announced the sale of shares in the Mohawk and Hudson Railroad. By 1831, this first rail line in New York opened for business between Albany and Schenectady. Its purpose was to move passengers on a direct 16-mile line between the two cities and to offer an alternative to the much slower 28-mile canal trip. At Schenectady, rail passengers journeying west were expected to board canal boats, and, ideally, the railroad was seen as a supplement, or compliment, to the canal, not a competitor.[44] Luring investors to buy stock in a company that could be construed as competing with New York's "Grand Canal" would have been difficult, if not impossible, anyway. Contemporary conventional wisdom cautioned that other forms of transportation could not stand up to the mighty Erie.

Early admonitions notwithstanding, it soon was apparent that railroads *would* challenge the supremacy of the Erie. In fact, after the Mohawk and Hudson's uproarious 47-minute initial run, New York politician and company director Churchill C. Cambreling toasted the new enterprise: "The Buffalo Rail Road—may we soon breakfast in Utica, dine at Rochester, and sup with our friends on Lake Erie."[45] Cambreling's insight proved accurate when, two years later, the Utica and Schenectady Railroad was incorporated. Its line closely paralleled the Erie Canal between the two cities. Although the New York Legislature took steps to protect its canal by prohibiting the Utica and Schenectady from carrying freight, the prohibition was softened after only eight years of railroad operation. In 1844, the legislature allowed freight on the Utica and Schenectady during the months that the Erie Canal was closed, but with the stipulation that the railroad pay the same tolls as would have been paid had the merchandise been carried on the canal.[46] This restriction, though, was dropped within a few years.

By 1843, seven railroads spanned the distance between Albany and Buffalo. Ten years later they were consolidated into the New York Central Railroad. The new road's connection with New York City was via the Hudson River Railroad or Hudson River steamboats. In 1851, two years prior to the formation of the New York Central, the completion of the New York and Erie Railroad offered a more direct connection from the lower Hudson Valley to Lake Erie. Both railroads challenged the supremacy of the Erie Canal as a link to the West, but it was not until the end of the 1860s that their combined tonnage surpassed that carried on the canal. Even then the canal edged out the New York Central in number of tons transported, since two-thirds of the railroad merchandise was carried on the New York and Erie.[47]

The Erie Canal's first enlargement was declared "completed" by the State in September 1862 at a cost of $31,834,041. It took more than three times as long to build the enlargement as it did to finish the original canal and the larger canal cost nearly 4½ times as much as "Clinton's Ditch."[48] One event that contributed to the delay was the legislature's passage in 1842 of the "Stop and Tax" law. This legislation halted new construction on the Erie Enlargement and the Genesee and Black River Canals, also in progress at the time. In brief, the act, passed by the Democrats who had

Above:

The Erie Canal in Clinton Square, Syracuse, looking east, c. 1903

The Weighlock Building, Syracuse, looking southeast across the Erie Canal, c. 1897. The building currently houses the Erie Canal Museum.

Overleaf:

A trip on the Erie Canal at Auriesville, looking southeast, c. 1890,

All courtesy of the Canal Society of New York State

gained control of the legislature, was aimed at the Whigs, who were accused of wasting the state's money on canal building. The law levied a tax to reduce state debt. Eventually, construction resumed on all canals.

There is no question that competition from railroads caused canal traffic to diminish. Yet, the Erie Canal had its greatest tonnage year in 1880—a half-century *after* railroads came to New York. Water transportation continued to be less expensive than shipping on iron roads, and the Erie Canal had firmly established itself in the race for western trade. Canal tonnage remained substantial throughout the remainder of the nineteenth century.

The Erie Canal's opening was a major gain for New York in the race to dominate trade with the West. The Erie's builders had an advantage in the water-level route through the Appalachian Mountains that other states and cities found impossible to overcome. As a result, the mighty Erie offered a connection to the nation's interior that could not be seriously challenged by any of the other contenders on the Atlantic Coast.

"A Busy Apple Season" along the Erie Canal in Medina, c. 1905.
Courtesy of the Canal Society of New York State

Then and Now:
Enlarged Erie Lock 52, Port Byron, looking east, c. 1900 and the lock today alongside the New York State Thruway, looking east, 1989.

Above: courtesy of the Canal Society of New York State
Below: courtesy of the New York State Museum

III. The Lateral Canals

THE ERIE CANAL was primarily responsible for creating the Albany-to-Buffalo population corridor, and it assisted in maintaining the urbanization of the Hudson Valley south of Albany. With the exception of Long Island's suburban sprawl, the New York City-to-Albany-to-Buffalo axes remain the focal residential areas of New York. After the Erie opened, the overwhelming success of the canal and its positive impact on the areas along its route were not lost on the people in the rest of the state. The result was that those not living on or near the canal wanted access to the Erie. State leaders responded by building several canals to connect New York's northern and southern tiers to the main line of the Erie. The new canals were called *laterals*.

At least one lateral canal was built not only to connect another part of the state with the Erie, but also to provide the Erie with an additional source of water. Canals are hydraulic structures, and they require a regular source of water to keep the water depth constant. Evaporation and seepage account for some water loss, but most of the loss occurs when boats are locked from one level to another—since the water flows from the higher elevation to the lower, it is lost from the upper level, and plentiful sources of water must be located at

Lateral canal locks on the Black River Canal.
Author's colleciton

higher elevations to replace the water that is wasted during lock operation. (Canals also can be fed from streams that flow parallel.) Because the Erie Canal was at a lower elevation than most laterals that connected to it, it could benefit from their waste water. The Black River Canal was built specifically with this as part of its purpose. Since the laterals required a constant supply of water as well, many of them had *feeder canals* to help provide it; frequently, feeders also were used as branch canals.

New York State's lateral canals can be divided into three groups according to their type and sequence of construction: those that were canalized improvements of existing natural waterways and eventually became part of the Barge Canal System (the Champlain, Oswego, and Cayuga and Seneca Canals); those that were constructed before the Erie Canal enlargement was authorized in 1835 but were not enlarged to

CARTHAGE
AND
NEW YORK.

1861.

THE BLACK RIVER AND NEW YORK LINE OF CANAL BOATS

Will contract for, receive and deliver Freight, to and from New York and Carthage, and all intermediate points on the Canals and the Black River,

AT REDUCED PRICES!

All Goods shipped by this Line are Insured.

The place of Shipment from New York will be

PIER No. 3, EAST RIVER.

Packages should be marked

"BLACK RIVER & NEW YORK LINE."

FOR FREIGHT APPLY TO

W. A. HORR, Carthage,
H. BLODGET, Denmark,
M. M. SMITH, Smith's Landing,
GEO. F. WATSON, Lowville Landing,
C. B. BEACH, Beaches Bridge,
CAPELL BROTHERS, Port Leyden,
P. MANN, New Bremen,

JAMES H. MALROY, New, York,
CHAMBERLAIN, Albany,
T. D. COLLINS, West Troy,
A. E. CULVER Utica,
J. CARLEY, Rome,
JOHSLYN & SHULTZ, Boonville,
M. COYL, Lyons Falls.

KOHLER, WHEELOCK & CO., Proprietors.

For Sale!

Flour, Feed, Salt, Plaster, Water Lime,

AND CEMENT,

At the Store House on the Dock, in Carthage.

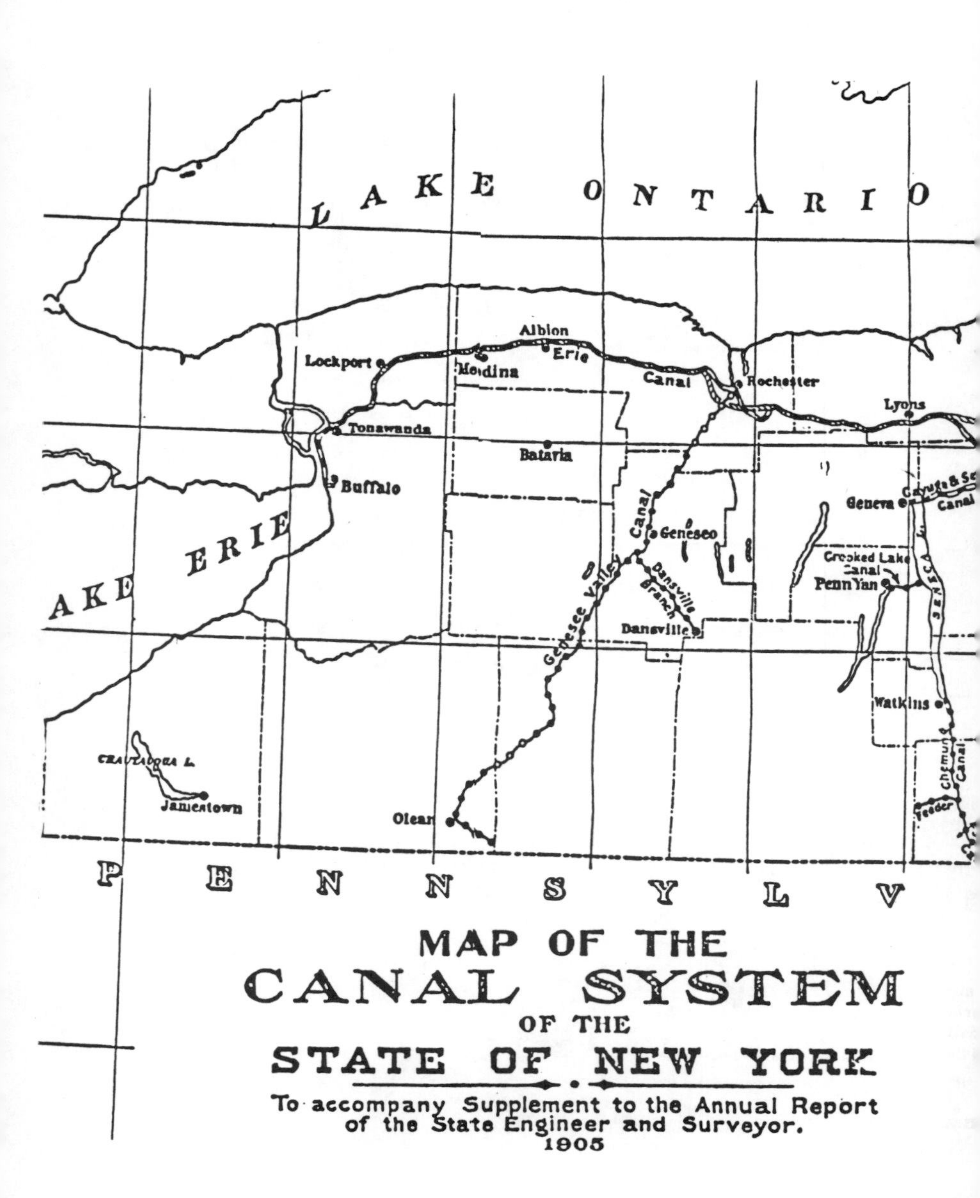
LAKE ONTARIO
Lockport
Albion
Medina
Erie
Canal
Rochester
Lyons
Tonawanda
Batavia
Buffalo
AKE ERIE
Canal
Geneseo
Genesee Valley
Dansville
Branch
Dansville
Geneva
Canal
Crooked Lake
Canal
Penn Yan
SENECA
Watkins
Chemung
Canal
Feeder
Olean
Jamestown
P E N N S Y L V
MAP OF THE
CANAL SYSTEM
OF THE
STATE OF NEW YORK
To accompany Supplement to the Annual Report
of the State Engineer and Surveyor.
1905

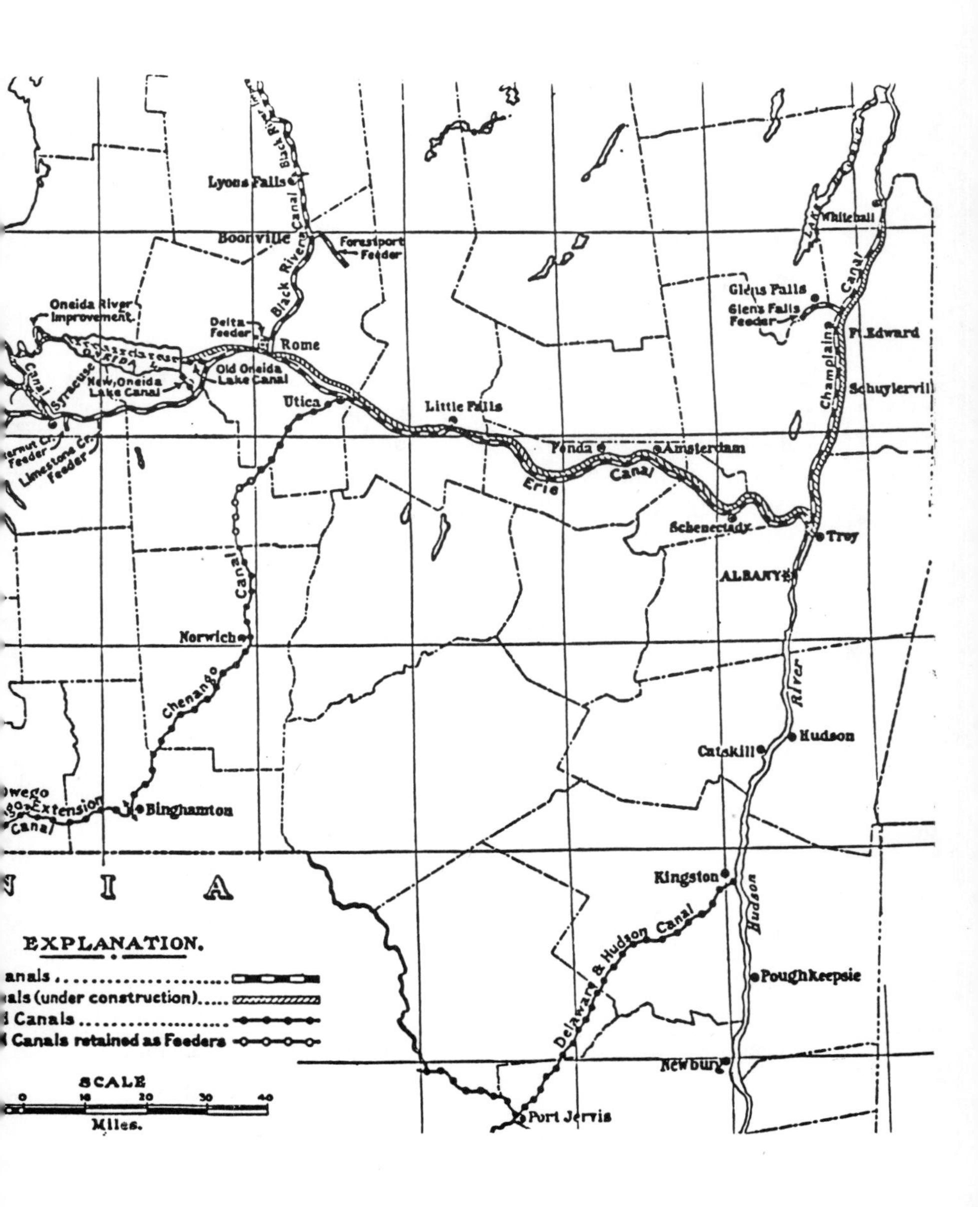

Lyons Falls
Black River Canal
Boonville
Forestport Feeder
Oneida River Improvement
Delta Feeder
Black River Canal
Rome
Old Oneida Lake Canal
New Oneida Lake Canal
Syracuse
Utica
Little Falls
Fonda
Amsterdam
Erie Canal
Schenectady
Troy
ALBANY
Whitehall
Lake Champlain
Glens Falls
Glens Falls Feeder
Ft. Edward
Champlain Canal
Schuylervill
Limestone Cr. Feeder
Chenango Canal
Norwich
Binghamton
Extension Canal
River
Hudson
Catskill
Kingston
Delaware & Hudson Canal
Hudson
Poughkeepsie
Newburg
Port Jervis
EXPLANATION.
Canals (under construction)
Canals retained as Feeders
SCALE
Miles.

the dimensions of the rebuilt Erie (the Chemung, Crooked Lake, Oneida Lake, and Chenango Canals), and those that were built later (the Genesee Valley and the Black River Canals). Although these last two canals were constructed after the Erie Enlargement was approved, they were built essentially to the dimensions of the original Erie, a shortsighted decision that limited the connectivity of the Genesee Valley and Black River Canals with the new Erie. In other words, the bigger boats of the enlarged Erie could not use the smaller canals.

Clearly the first group of laterals were the most successful in terms of tonnage carried and tolls collected. When an 1882 state referendum abolished tolls on state-operated canals, the Champlain, Oswego, and Cayuga and Seneca Canals ranked second, third, and fourth behind the Erie in toll dollars. Only those four canals were incorporated into the state's Barge Canal System in the twentieth century.

Champlain Canal

NEW YORK STATE is blessed with two natural water-level routes from the Hudson River in the Albany area. In addition to the Mohawk's way west, 125-mile-long Lake Champlain leads the way to the north. Bordering on Vermont and Canada, the lake makes up approximately two-thirds of the distance from Albany to Montreal and the St. Lawrence River. Native Americans had traveled the lake for centuries, and when the Europeans arrived they began using the convenient route as well. In 1609, Samuel de Champlain, with two other Frenchmen and a number of Native Americans, voyaged southward in the lake that now bears his name. Champlain and his party may have ventured as far south as what is now Glens Falls before returning to Canada. When England and France began their long struggle for control of much of North America by the end of the seventeenth century, the Champlain route was used and fought over during four wars between the two nations. So important was the passage that the French built a powerful stone fort at Ticonderoga in 1757; much of it can still be seen today.

The military use of New York's northern water route continued during the Revolution, when an American army advanced through it in an unsuccessful invasion of Canada. Two years later, in 1777, a British force descended into New York via Lake Champlain on a campaign that was stopped by the decisive American victory at Saratoga. Then again, in 1814, the British invaded from Canada using Lake Champlain, but this time they were halted by the Americans at Plattsburgh in both land and water battles. The victory over the British fleet at Plattsburgh led to the end of the War of 1812.

Two decades before the beginning of that war, the Northern Inland Lock Navigation Company planned to improve the northern water route similar to the way the Western Inland Lock Navigation Company had developed the state's western waterways. The company secured the services of a French engineer, Marc I. Brunel, to supervise the construction. Although Brunel was competent and apparently conducted some preliminary surveys, little was accomplished and the project failed. It was not until 1812 that the state's canal commissioners noted that "a canal between Lake Champlain and Hudson's river is one of those things which are deemed of national importance."[49] The war served to substantiate their observation.

The commissioners followed up on their report in March 1817, when they stressed to the legislature the advantages of a canal to Lake Champlain. They noted that the region of Lake Champlain and the 32-mile-long Lake George (located nearby to the southwest) abounded in valuable timber, and to the west of Lake Champlain were extensive and rich deposits of iron. Both commodities could be inexpensively shipped by canal, as could high-quality Vermont marble.[50]

On April 15, 1817—the same day that the Erie Canal construction was authorized—the Champlain Canal was approved. Work commenced soon after, with James Geddes of Erie Canal notoriety conducting the final route survey. The canal's dimensions were the same as those of the original Erie. A total of 19 lift locks were built to negotiate the change in elevation in the 66 miles between Waterford and Whitehall on Lake Champlain. Construction was completed on September 23,1823, at a cost of $921,011, only $50,000 more than the engineer's estimate.[51]

Horatio Gates Spafford, author of New York gazetteers, witnessed and described the festival held by the people of Waterford and Lansingburgh (Troy) to mark the opening of the canal. A fleet, including steam boats, arrived amid cannon fire, bell ringing, music playing, and cheers of the assembly who enthusiastically greeted the new waterway. Spafford speculated on how unusual it would be "to see the voyagers of Canada. . .navigating the Hudson, every oar keeping time to the wild notes and melodious cadences of the Canadian Boat Song," and to watch "Canadian Indians, paddling along in their bark canoes, having come from the terra borealis of North America! and then by-and-by, there will be no novelty in all this!"[52] Apparently, Spafford still considered the sight of canoes novel when he observed at the gala opening "an Indian canoe of birch bark, from Canada, darting and dodging about, [among the larger boats] like the hum-bird among the tenants of the air."[53]

The Champlain Canal was an instant success: More than 19,000 boats passed through it during its first year.[54] It was second only to the Erie Canal in tons of goods carried and total amount of tolls collected.[55] As canal historian Ronald Shaw points out, the Champlain Canal took "the major share of the trade of western Massachusetts and Vermont" and directed it to New York City by way of the Hudson River. Shaw facetiously refers to the Champlain as "New England's greatest canal."[56]

Oswego Canal

THE WESTERNMOST PART of the old trade link from Albany followed Wood Creek from the Great Carrying Place (Rome) to Oneida Lake, across the lake to its outlet, the Oneida River, through the winding ten miles of river to its junction with the Seneca River, where the two streams became the Oswego River, then 20 miles downstream to Lake Ontario at Oswego. Founded by the British as a fort and trading post in the mid-1720s, Oswego was important enough to be the site of conflict between the British and French during the French and Indian War in the 1750s. In the American Revolution 20 years later, British forces launched part of their campaign of 1777 from Oswego; the Royal army marched east along the trail to Fort Stanwix (Rome) where they were turned back by the Americans. The British fell back to Oswego but refused to leave when the war ended in 1783. This left them in control of the western terminus of the trade route, where they were free to block trade and menace travelers. One example of this was an incident involving three French citizens traveling to the Black River region (Jefferson County) in October 1793. They were halted and narrowly escaped being held prisoner by the British as they attempted to pass through Oswego. When threatened by the fort's commandant, the French responded that they were allies of the Americans and "could go upon the territory of their allies. . .and that [they] had no intentions of going to Canada, but to the Black River, which belonged to the State of New York, as did also the Oswego Country."[57] The British abandoned Oswego three years later under the terms of the Jay Treaty.

Shortly thereafter, Oswego's importance was enhanced by the completion of the Western Inland Lock Navigation Company's waterway improvements between Albany and Oneida Lake. Later, when a route for the Erie Canal was under study, Oswego was considered as a logical western terminus, but the Lake Ontario connection evaporated when it was decided that a canal built directly to Lake Erie would not be as vulnerable to Canadian influence or to the possibility of attack if another war broke out between the United States and Britain.

Once construction on the Erie Canal was in progress, however, a link to Lake Ontario that would capture the trade coming from the residents near the lake on both sides of the international border was considered. With the exception of the people of Rochester, who wanted the junction made there, there was considerable support for the Oswego line. The incorporation of the Oswego Canal Company in 1823 helped the choice of that route, but so little was actually accomplished by the company that the state took over in 1825.[58] The Oswego Canal was scheduled for completion under state direction in time for a spring 1828 opening. But a severe outbreak of fever incapacitated so many laborers that work was not finished until December, and the commencement of traffic was delayed until April 28, 1829.[59]

The Oswego Canal cost less than $600,000 to build. Nearly half of its 38 miles was slack water in the Oswego River. The river was maintained at the necessary level by dams, and a towpath was constructed along the bank. The required 18 lift locks were the same dimensions as those on the Erie Canal, as was the Oswego's prism, or ditch.[60]

The Oswego Canal was second only to the Erie in number of boat clearances (an indication of canal usage) during the 25 years after it opened.[61] Undoubtedly this was an important reason why, unlike many of the other lateral canals, the Oswego later was rebuilt to the same dimensions as those of the enlarged Erie Canal. The expanded Oswego was declared finished the same day as the Erie enlargement, September 1, 1862.[62] Changes made to the Oswego Canal helped keep its overall volume of trade behind only the Champlain Canal among the laterals.[63] Like the Champlain, it continues in operation.

Cayuga and Seneca Canal

THE FINGER LAKES REGION of west-central New York contains most of the narrow, north-south lakes that give the area its name. The two largest lakes are the 38-mile-long Cayuga, and its neighbor ten miles to the west, the 35-mile-long Seneca. These two large lakes offer access to a sizable territory, and their value as avenues of trade are supplemented by the Seneca River, which flows from the northern end of Seneca Lake east until it joins with the Oneida to form the Oswego River. As early as 1792, the Western Inland Lock Navigation Company's charter included the right to improve navigation along the watercourse to Seneca Lake. But the company's efforts never extended beyond Oneida Lake, and in 1808 it relinquished its rights west of the lake.

Five years later in 1813, residents of Seneca County petitioned the legislature to improve a portion of the water route. That same year, the Seneca Lock Navigation Company was incorporated to complete a navigable connection between the two largest Finger Lakes. Shortage of funds slowed the work, forcing the state to contribute about 30 percent of the $70,000 needed to finish. The opening from Seneca to Cayuga Lake came in 1821,[64] when the Erie Canal was under construction. A petition to the legislature in 1824 by the people of nine Finger Lake counties sought state improvements in the existing Cayuga and Seneca waterways and a connection with the Erie Canal at Montezuma. The following year the state authorized acquisition of the Seneca Lock Navigation Company; David Thomas, an Erie Canal engineer, was appointed to conduct a line survey for the new canal.

Construction of the 22-mile canal got under way in 1826. Its prism and lock dimensions were identical to those of the original Erie Canal, but its 12 lift locks were made of wood instead of stone.[65] (Wood was plentiful in upstate New York; this was not the first time it had been used as lock material.) About half of the distance of the Cayuga and Seneca was slack-water navigation using the natural channel of the Seneca River. The canal, from Seneca Lake at Geneva to the Erie Canal at Montezuma, took a little over two years to complete and opened on November 15, 1828.[66]

Within a few years, the people of the region began to push for an enlargement of their canal when it became known that the Erie Canal's dimensions would be expanded. Initial approval for the increase in lock size came in 1836, when the Erie enlargement was authorized. But delays prevented the start of work, and in 1847 permission was again given to build the Erie-size locks: 110 by 18 feet. The new locks were not completed until 1854, the same year as the prism was enlarged to 70 feet wide by 7 feet deep, also the size of the new Erie. The final cost of construction usually was considerably higher than the engineer's estimate, but in this case the $1,133,149 total expense was only $321,961 over the initial calculation.[67] Like the Champlain and the Oswego, this canal is still in operation.

Chemung Canal

SOME OF NEW YORK'S NUMEROUS RIVERS flow south from the southern tier into Pennsylvania. The Chemung River is among them. Formed by the confluence of the Canisteo and

Cohocton Rivers at Painted Post, its 41 miles flow toward its junction with the Susquehanna River a short distance beyond the state line. In 1779, during the Revolution, Generals John Sullivan and James Clinton led an American force into western New York. Sullivan, impressed with the fertility of the Chemung region, passed along his observations to George Washington with the recommendation that an artificial waterway be built to connect with Pennsylvania. Although there was substantial migration into the Chemung Valley after the war, Sullivan's advice was not acted upon until the early nineteenth century.

In 1812, James Geddes investigated the route as directed by the canal commissioners, and he supported improving the area's natural waterways. Three years later, residents of the region urged the construction of the improvements; they wanted changes made in order to facilitate the movement of local products, such as salt and plaster of Paris, to markets in Pennsylvania. An initial result was the incorporation of the Seneca and Susquehanna Lock Navigation Company, capitalized at $300,000, to connect Seneca Lake with the Chemung River in Tioga (now Chemung) County. The act of incorporation specified canal prism and lock dimensions and stipulated completion of the project within 14 years. But little was accomplished.[68]

By 1825 interest in the canal was renewed, and James Geddes again was called upon to make a survey. The following year he reported to the legislature that an 18-mile-long canal should be built from Seneca Lake directly south to Newtown in Chemung County, which, in addition to 13 miles of navigable feeder, would total 31 canal miles. Geddes estimated the construction cost at $240,000 using wooden locks, or $407,598 with stone locks. The debate following in the legislature was influenced by the fact that the building of the Cayuga and Seneca Canal was underway, and the proposed Chemung waterway was seen as an extension creating a 78-mile-long access to the Erie. Also, the operators of the salt industry in Syracuse saw the connection to Pennsylvania as a way to import coal to replace the dwindling local wood supply needed to process their salt.

Finally, the canal was approved in 1829, and engineer Holmes Hutchinson quickly began work. The population of the region, especially the people of Elmira, was ecstatic.[69] Hutchinson's cost estimate was $331,125 for a prism two feet wider than the original Erie, and for 49 wooden lift locks. Building started in 1830 and was finished in 1833 at a figure almost $17,000 less than the estimate.[70] The completed canal ran 39 miles—at $8,505 per mile the least expensive of the state canals.[71]

As expected, the people of Elmira were overjoyed with the canal's completion, and "a boat load of celebrants went up [the canal] as far as Pine Valley, having added to their number others from Horseheads and on the way. The boat used was a scow" that usually carried building stone. It was so crowded that "all had to stand up, but the enjoyment was great at the cost of a 'shilling' [12.5¢] a head. A great many flags were flying; there were speeches and songs, and much genuine rejoicing."[72] Unfortunately the rejoicing turned out to be premature; a serious flood in May 1833 carried away 100 feet of feeder embankment, undermined locks, and washed out banks on the main canal. Extensive repair efforts allowed the canal to reopen the following October.

The initial years of the canal's operation did not meet expectations—annual tonnage failed to surpass the 100,000 mark until 1845.[73] Among the problems was the rapid deterioration of the wooden locks. Such was their condition that in 1839 the canal commissioners ordered an inspection, completed early in 1840. As a result of the engineer's report, new locks were ordered. But, of the four plans under consideration, the least expensive one—calling for replacement with timber locks at $4,390 each—was adopted. Work on the locks was finished by the opening of the 1843 season.[74]

The Chemung Canal's new locks lasted only about as long as the original ones, and by 1850 they were again in need of rebuilding. No immediate action was taken until 1853 when, due to a substantial increase in canal traffic, it was decided to construct reinforced wooden locks, as well as a few of wood-and-stone composition. This round of rebuilding was not finished until 1867. By then, the canal's greatest tonnage year—1863, when shipments exceeded 300,000 tons—had passed, and tonnage declined through the late-1860s and early-1870s.[75] Area railroads were taking their toll, and it became clear that the canal could not compete with them.

In 1846, during the height of the canal era, New York adopted a new constitution mandating the state's canals remain New York property forever. "Forever" turned out to be 28 years for many of the laterals. In 1874, voters approved a constitutional amendment that permitted the disposal of most of the canals, excepting the Erie, Oswego, Champlain, and Cayuga and Seneca.[76] This led to the closing and sale of many canals by 1878, including the Chemung Canal, except the ditch from Seneca Lake to Montour Falls.

Crooked Lake Canal

CROOKED LAKE, or Keuka Lake as it is more often called today, is located in Yates and Steuben Counties. Shaped like a fork, the eastern tine is roughly parallel to and about six miles west of Seneca Lake. At the upper end of that part of Keuka Lake is the village of Penn Yan. It is nearly 20 miles from there to Hammandsport at the lake's southern tip.

Once approval was given in 1825 to build the Cayuga and Seneca Canal, the people who lived near Crooked Lake wanted their own waterway access to the Erie. In 1827, residents of Yates County applied to the legislature to connect Crooked Lake with Seneca Lake and listed the benefit to area farming as their principal rationale. Although state lawmakers initially ignored the request, the next year they directed the canal commissioners to make surveys. Engineer David Thomas proposed a canal line that would connect Penn Yan with Dresden, 270 feet lower, on Seneca Lake. In April 1829, the commissioners received the legislature's nod to build the canal large enough for the passage of Erie Canal boats.[77]

Veteran engineer Holmes Hutchinson was chosen to carry out the work, which specifically forbade construction unless the waterway could be built for $120,000. Although the engineer's estimate was $800 under the limit, it did not take into consideration costs of other related improvements. Thus, the final expenditure when the canal was completed in October 1833 was nearly $27,000 more than the approved figure, though when compared with cost overruns on other state canals the excess was relatively minor.

That the project exceeded the budget limit came as no surprise to the canal commissioners, who described a number of abuses that they attributed to "overexploitation of the canal policy as it related to costly laterals." The commissioners realized the Crooked Lake Canal revenue would not equal its construction cost plus annual maintenance,[78] which was accurate. The canal's total income of $46,000 during its 42 years of operation was less than one-third the amount it cost to build it.[79] Nothing was left for its maintenance.

The Crooked Lake Canal's income surpassed $1,000 only during half of its total years in operation and topped $2,000 for just three of those years.[80] Clearly, what kept the canal in operation was the provision in the State Constitution of 1846 against canal abandonment. By the early 1870s, growing sentiment against spending public money to perpetuate costly canals reversed the earlier euphoria during the canal-building boom.

An example of the Crooked Lake Canal's financial deficiency can be found in the report of an investigative commission in 1875, the final year of operation. The investigators listed income from tolls at $126.09 for that year, against expenses of $7,710.15.[81] Closing of the canal awaited only enactment of the constitutional amendment passed by the voters in 1874. The Crooked Lake Canal was formally abandoned on June 4, 1877.

Oneida Lake Canal

A "CANAL" TO ONEIDA LAKE had existed at least since the first decade of the nineteenth century. As early as 1803, Benjamin Wright supervised construction of wooden locks and short canals built to eliminate sharp bends in Wood Creek. The work was undertaken by the Western Inland Lock Navigation Company as part of its effort to improve navigation between its canal at Rome and Oneida Lake. When the state began the Erie Canal, it purchased the company's works, and the improvements of the Western Inland Navigation Company were abandoned. Since the Erie Canal did not enter Oneida Lake, lakeside residents and those living along Wood Creek were deprived of a direct outlet for their produce and they turned to the state for help.

In 1832, the legislature incorporated the Oneida Lake Canal Company, capitalized at $40,000. The company was permitted to construct and operate a canal from the Erie Canal to Oneida Lake for 50 years. The toll rates could not exceed three times the toll charged on the Erie, and any time during the first ten years the state could take possession of the canal after compensating the company.

The Oneida Lake Canal, built to the Erie's dimensions, ran from the Erie Canal at Higginsville, four and one-half miles to Wood Creek, where it entered the creek for the two miles to Oneida Lake. A tow path was constructed along the creek's south bank. Seven wooden lift locks were built in addition to a guard lock where the canal entered Wood Creek. A total of $78,825 was spent on the canal, including the cost to build a three-mile-long feeder to contribute water to the Erie equal to that taken off by the Oneida Lake Canal. Navigation opened in late summer 1835.[82]

After only two years of operation, area residents complained that the Oneida Lake Canal Company's tolls were too high, and they pleaded for relief from the state. Their pleas went unheeded until 1839, when it became clear that the company was not fulfilling the terms of its charter. The company had promised to take water it needed from the Erie only equal to that provided by the feeder, but an investigation revealed that nearly twice as much water went into the Oneida Lake Canal from the Erie as was put back by the feeder. This revelation, plus renewed pressure on the legislature for a state takeover, resulted in a public purchase on April 12, 1841. The Oneida Lake Canal Company received $50,000, along with the state's guarantee that it would maintain the canal. With the purchase, tolls were reduced to the amount charged on other state-operated canals.[83]

Not only was the Oneida Lake Canal kept open, eventually it was enlarged. Soon after the state buyout, the Stop and Tax Law took effect, which restricted canal expenditures to maintenance only. But at the same time, tonnage on the Oneida Lake Canal began to increase, peaking from 1847 through 1854. This greater utilization wore down the canal structures, however, and by the mid-1850s the wooden locks were so dilapidated that it became increasingly difficult to keep the canal open. By 1862 it was nearly impassable. The lock chambers had narrowed from earth heaving against the lock walls during winter freezing and thawing. The canal was closed to traffic.[84]

Five years later, the Oneida Lake Canal was rejuvenated with passage of a law to build an enlarged canal along a new route. After much discussion, at the end of 1867 contracts were let for a canal from Durhamville, on the Erie Canal, to Oneida Lake's South Bay. The dimensions would be those of the enlarged Erie—70 feet wide by 7 feet deep, with masonry locks measuring 110 by 18 feet.

The New Oneida Lake Canal was only five and one-third miles long, but it took an incredible ten years to complete because of inadequate funding and cost overruns. When the canal finally was opened early in October 1877, breaks resulted in its closing after only about a month. The canal did not reopen until July 1, 1878, after which it was again plagued by numerous breaks, mainly attributed to quicksand in the soil.[85] At the end of the 1878 navigation season, the New Oneida Lake Canal was closed for good. The nearly $450,000 spent on construction was never recovered. Area residents, again cut off from a direct route to the Erie, remained so until the opening of the Barge Canal in 1918, which entered Oneida Lake and utilized the 21-mile-long lake as part of its route across New York State.

Chenango Canal

THE CHENANGO RIVER flows in a southerly direction out of the hills near Utica, to Binghamton, where it joins the Susquehanna River. Residents of the Chenango Valley felt they had a natural route for a canal to link with the Erie and agitated for one. Their eventual success was due largely to John Tracy, a valley man on the Democratic ticket for lieutenant governor in 1832. A Democratic victory that year prompted Governor William Marcy to recommend building a canal in his

1833 message to the legislature. An act passed the following month authorizing construction of a waterway from Binghamton along the Chenango River to its headwaters, and then by the most advantageous route to the Erie Canal.

John B. Jervis was chosen chief engineer, in part because of his experience building the Delaware and Hudson, a coal-carrying canal that ran from northeastern Pennsylvania to the Hudson River. Although he was aware that the canal commissioners reported the Chenango had little promise of commercial success, Jervis approached the job with the same diligence that he would have accorded a more important assignment.[86]

Building the Chenango Canal posed two major problems. The first was the choice of a route from the Chenango River headwaters to the Erie Canal. Ultimately this was settled in 1834, when state lawmakers, bowing to pressure from Utica, ruled that the city should be the northern terminus. The second and more difficult problem was finding an adequate water source for the summit level at Hamilton. The Chenango Canal was an interbasin canal, that is, it connected two separate watersheds. Jervis' solution was the use of reservoirs, even though skeptics predicted they would not work; experience showed that the artificial lakes would retain insufficient water. Jervis constructed a rain gauge that indicated the reservoirs would keep 40 percent of the rainfall, a sufficient amount. Seven reservoirs eventually were built on the summit level, which not only supplied the Chenango, but helped furnish water for the Rome level of the Erie Canal. Jervis' measurement of rainfall and runoff serves as a hallmark in the history of American hydrology.[87]

Although building went ahead as scheduled, it became necessary for contractors to increase wages in order to attract and keep workers. During the spring of 1834, pay went from $11 to $15 a month due to increased labor demand in the Midwest, where a frenzy of canal digging was in progress.[88]

Workers on the line, many of whom were Irish, mirrored those on other state canals under construction in the 1830s and 1840s. They worked hard, after which many enjoyed their own form of entertainment. The *Hamilton Republican* reported in 1834 that at night and on Sundays, "the wildest of drunken revelry and desperate pugilistic encounters was the only enjoyment [the workers] seemed to care for." Whiskey flowed so freely that it was said rubber boots could have been sold if they were available to wear in the Hamilton saloons.[89] In one instance, four militia companies were mobilized to quell a labor strike near Deansboro, in Oneida County. The opening victory went to the laborers' wives, who swung stockings filled with stones and drove back the troops. But by day's end the militia prevailed and the strike leaders were in custody.[90]

All 97 miles and 116 lift locks of the canal were completed by October 1836, at a cost of $2.3 million, only somewhat above the initial estimate.[91] The canal opened the following spring. True to earlier predictions, coal was an important freight. Some boats were used only on the Chenango Canal to haul coal from Binghamton to the Franklin Iron Works in Franklin Springs, near Utica. Pig iron made the return trip.[92] In the late 1840s, coal also was shipped to three steam-powered cotton mills that had opened in Utica.

But coal was not the sole cargo on the canal. Some 20,000 barrels of cider per year and large numbers of hop bales were carried from the Bouckville level. In 1859, nearly all hops grown in the United States were from New York State, with the middle region along the Western Turnpike (U.S. Route 20) the center of production.[93] People rode the Chenango Canal, as well; among the important passengers were the thousand men of the 114th New York Infantry, who left Norwich on ten canal boats early in September 1862. When the Civil War ended in 1865, just 456 men returned by canal.[94]

In 1863, the legislature authorized the building of a 40-mile Chenango Canal Extension west of Binghamton along the south bank of the Susquehanna River to the Pennsylvania border. The plan was to connect with Pennsylvania's North Branch Canal to facilitate coal shipments. Unfortunately, the authorization did not include an appropriation to cover construction costs and the project languished. It was abandoned with the ditch extending about three-quarters of the total distance a decade later. The Binghamton, Dunshore and Williamsport Railroad was given permission to lay track on the extension's tow path, but even that never occurred.[95]

It was insufficient traffic that sealed the fate of the Chenango. During only five of the 39 years the canal was open were more than 100,000 tons carried on its boats. The peak year was 1868, when cargo totaled 112,000 tons.[96] Lack of traffic substantiated the earlier warning that the Chenango would not be a commercial success. But the Chenango suffered the same handicap as many of the laterals. It was not enlarged to the new dimensions of the Erie, which prevented use by the larger boats. Also, like other lateral canals, the Chenango was hurt by competition from railroads. The result: The Chenango Canal closed on May 1, 1878.

Genesee Valley Canal

THE GENESEE RIVER flows north from New York's southern tier and empties into Lake Ontario at Rochester. About 30 miles south of Rochester, its valley broadens into the rich,

Facing Page:

The Genesee Valley Canal hugging the hillside in Letchworth Gorge, c. 1870.

Courtesy of the Canal Society of New York State

rolling plain that attracted soldiers of the 1779 Sullivan-Clinton Expedition. Even before the Revolution ended, veterans began returning as settlers to the region. By the time the Erie Canal was completed, the Genesee Valley was one of the principal wheat-producing areas of the state. While the Erie was under construction, residents of the valley saw an opportunity to open a commercial route from the Erie at Rochester to the Ohio River. A canal constructed southward through the Genesee Valley, across a narrow divide to Olean, could access the Allegheny River, which flows into the Ohio, and could tap a huge portion of trans-Appalachian America. A petition to build the canal went to the legislature in 1823, but to no avail.[97]

During the next 13 years, pressure for a canal continued unabated, including support from as far away as New York City. The legislature finally responded positively in 1836 and approved a canal from Rochester south to Mt. Morris, then by the best route to the Allegheny River near Olean. Engineer Frederick C. Mills estimated construction cost at $2,002,285, which included an 18-mile branch canal to Dansville. The main canal was 107 miles long, with dimensions nearly identical to those of the first Erie Canal. The Genesee Valley Canal's 104 lift locks of stone, wood, and a composite of both overcame an elevation difference of 1,128 feet.[98]

By 1841, the line from Rochester to the Dansville branch, including the branch canal, was completed. With 52 miles in operation, work was halted between 1842 and 1847. This resulted from the legislature's worry that too much money was being spent on canals, and the Stop and Tax Law was passed to stop letting contracts and to levy a tax to reduce the state debt. When building started again, a cut 73 feet deep and a series of 17 lift locks were needed to get from the Cashagua Valley to the Genesee Valley. When construction crews were within two miles of Portageville, they were confronted by a high rock ridge, and in places excavation was necessary to a depth of 60 feet in solid rock. As the cut deepened, engineers decided to tunnel instead. Nearly $250,000 was spent in a heroic attempt to drill, blast, and dig a hole 1,082 feet long—without success. The tunnel was abandoned in favor of building around the hill.[99]

Going around the ridge instead of through it presented nearly as much of an obstacle. After considerable labor, the builders succeeded "in pinning the Canal to the treacherous side of the towering mountain" with "a narrow strip of land alone [serving] as a towpath from which the descent was almost perpendicular to the river."[100] Little wonder that, as completed to Olean in 1857, the Genesee Valley Canal cost $5,663,184, or almost three times the original estimate.[101]

Nonetheless, the canal was of some value. It helped carry much of the 25,000 bushels of wheat used daily by the Rochester flour mills; it brought oil to Rochester from the wells of Pennsylvania; and it was a challenging training ground for engineers. The Genesee Valley Canal's greatest tonnage year was in 1854, when 5,345 boats cleared the first lock south of Rochester to move a record 158,942 tons.[102] But cargoes surpassed 100,000 tons for only a third of the years of the canal's operation.[103] Total revenues amounted to a little over $860,000, against maintenance and repair costs of $2,815,000.[104] Added to this $2 million loss was the fact that the canal generated nothing toward paying its cost of construction.

The Genesee Valley Canal's poor fiscal balance sheet, coupled with its numerous landslides and washouts, resulted in its final closing in September 1878.

Black River Canal

THE BLACK RIVER CANAL remained in operation longer than any of the lateral canals except those incorporated into the

Barge Canal System. It was built from the Erie Canal at Rome, north to the Black River at Lyon's Falls (called High Falls at the time of construction). From there, commerce followed the river through Carthage and Watertown west to Lake Ontario. The canal between Rome and Boonville, along the eastern fringe of the Tug Hill Plateau, was described by Shaw as "a dramatic feat of canal engineering."[105]

In 1825, the people of Herkimer, Oneida, Lewis, and Jefferson Counties petitioned the state legislature to build a canal connecting the Black River with the Erie Canal. Arguments for a canal extolled the Black River Valley as one of the most fertile parts of the state, with a substantial population, abundant valuable timber, and good-quality iron ore.[106] But getting the Black River Valley's two principal products to East Coast markets was both difficult and costly. For example, a valley wheat farmer of the 1820s likely chose from among three shipping routes to New York City. One was down the Black River to Lake Ontario, through the lake to the St. Lawrence River, and downriver to the Atlantic Ocean. (The direct distance from the Black River Valley to New York City is approximately 250 miles, but via the Atlantic it is more than eight times as long.) The second, shorter route used the Black River, Lake Ontario, and the St. Lawrence as far as Montreal; from Montreal, the wheat went south through the Richelieu River and Lake Champlain to the Champlain Canal (opened in 1823), then down the Hudson River to New York City. (The use of either of these itineraries meant that the cargo passed through Canadian waters, which could have added a tariff.) The third alternative involved the

Facing Page:

Locks and aqueduct at the Lake Delta Dam. Black River Canal, c. 1910-1915.

Author's collection

shortest distance, but an expensive overland shipment through the rugged Lansing Kill gorge from Boonville to Rome; once at Rome, the wheat could have been loaded on an Erie Canal boat for New York City. Since much of the Black River country's produce included bulk items, the use of the Erie Canal route was economically out of the question until a connecting canal was constructed.

In 1828, the legislature approved surveys of three possible canal routes. James Geddes was hired for the job. Based on his report, the 35-mile line chosen went from Rome, through Boonville, to Lyon's Falls, and involved 1,122 feet of lockage.[107] It was decided to let private enterprise build the canal, and thus the Black River Canal Company was incorporated, with a capitalization of $400,000. The company was allowed three years to construct a canal "of suitable width and dimensions" (to be determined by the company) from Rome to Lyon's Falls. Unfortunately, the Black River Canal Company exhausted its resources in preliminary surveys and planning, and made no other progress.[108]

The company's demise led to the 1832 incorporation of the Black River Company, with double the capital of the earlier corporation. This time, the legislature stipulated that only a portion of the project need be done in three years and, if so, another ten years could be used to finish. But at the end of three years the second company also went defunct. It became obvious that the only way to get a canal to the Black River Valley was for the state to build it, and, with support from Governor William Marcy, a construction bill passed in 1836.[109]

Work on the Black River Canal began in 1838, with engineer Porteus Root estimating construction cost at $2,069,562. The 35-mile excavated portion was 42 feet wide at the surface and 4 feet deep. It contained 109 lift locks, for an average of 15 locks per five miles of canal. (The Erie Canal enlargement, under construction simultaneously, averaged only one lock per five miles of canal.) To allow for navigation of the Black River, 42 miles were dredged from Lyon's Falls to Carthage.[110]

Construction was halted in 1842 on the Black River and Genesee Valley canals, as well as on the Erie enlargement, due to the Stop and Tax Law. With building at a standstill, many of the immigrant Irish laborers on the Black River and on the Erie Canal enlargement returned to agricultural pursuits, but could afford only inexpensive, marginal farmland. Those who attempted to farm the Tug Hill Plateau in the vicinity of Highmarket, near the Black River Valley, could not sustain themselves on the poor land. By the beginning of the twentieth century, their experiment ended; most had abandoned their farms and drifted to Mohawk Valley cities in search of factory work.[111]

Although some work on the canal resumed in 1848, it was not until 1851 that full construction was again under way. Simultaneously, the Black River was deepened in order to allow navigation to Lake Ontario; dams, jetties, and pilings also were used to help insure that the river would remain navigable. The Black River Canal and its Forestport feeder were completed in November 1855 at a final cost of $3,157,296, or $1 million above the original estimate. The question remained whether the canal would ever pay for the high cost of construction plus maintenance, and benefit the region.[112]

The chief hindrance to economical canal operation was breaks in the earthen walls or banks, which were easily washed away. On the Black River Canal, washouts most frequently took place in the Lansing Kill gorge, where in some places the canal was 100 feet above the stream bottom. Yet, on July 23, 1897, it was not in that gorge, but near Forestport that one of the worst breaks in canal history occurred, when 400 feet of towpath bank went out. A force of 1,700 men labored 30 days to repair the break. The reconstruction cost $62,782, with laborers receiving $1.65 per day and each of the 250 teams bringing 35¢ an hour to their owners. The massive break was followed by two others at practically the same spot. Vandalism was suspected and Pinkerton detectives were called in; through their efforts, nearly a score of men were arrested.[113]

When the Black River Canal opened in 1851, 23,320 tons of freight moved through it. Commerce on the canal peaked in 1889, with a total of 143,561 tons, but three years later dropped to 115,469 tons and by 1894 fell to 56,024 tons. (The sharp decline of 1894 undoubtedly reflected the impact of the disastrous depression of 1893.) Although a slight recovery occurred by 1900, the first two decades of the twentieth century saw less and less canal use, except for a spurt of

Rebuilding a lock on the Black River Canal near Boonville, c. 1890.

Courtesy of the Canal Society of New York State

activity during construction of Delta Lake, north of Rome, as a feeder for the new Barge Canal.[114]

Aside from railroad competition, depletion of the area's natural resources also contributed to the canal's decline. In 1893, wood and wood products valued at approximately $880,000 accounted for nearly 94 percent of the 54,781 tons of goods that passed through Boonville. By 1902, wood and wood products made up only 38 percent of the 76,569 tons carried on the canal; stone, lime, and clay were 61 percent of the tonnage. The value of canal shipments in 1902 was about half what is was in 1893. It became clear that the area served by the Black River Canal no longer could support the waterway.

The end finally came on July 24, 1924, when the state scow was let down from Boonville to Rome. This routine act ended operations on a canal that served the people of the Black River valley for over 70 years.[115] Only the Forestport Feeder continues to supply water to the existing canal system. The canal ditch between Rome and Boonville traverses a rugged and remote region, one reason why most of its structures still stand.

Lumber boat on the Black River Canal.

Author's collection

IV. The Corporate Canals

Delaware and Hudson Canal

THE DELAWARE AND HUDSON CANAL COMPANY was the most successful among New York's corporate canal builders. An important factor contributing to its success was that three prominent engineers all lent their talents to the company's canal during its first quarter century: Benjamin Wright, John B. Jervis, and John Roebling .

The Delaware and Hudson Company was organized in 1825 under the leadership of Philadelphia merchants William and Maurice Wurts. They owned coal lands in northeastern Pennsylvania and faced the problem of transporting anthracite from the mines to eastern urban markets. In order to raise the needed capital, the Wurts brothers sought help in New York City; they even brought coal samples to the Tontine Coffee House on Wall Street to demonstrate its fuel value. Prominent New Yorkers purchased stock in the company, and in 1825 New York City mayor Philip Hone was named its first president, and Benjamin Wright its chief engineer.[116]

The route chosen by Wright took the canal from Honesdale, Pennsylvania, along the Lackawaxen Creek and the Delaware River to what is now Port Jervis, New York, then northeasterly to Kingston, on the Hudson River. For construction purposes the project was divided into two parts: a

"Mechanical Methods of Handling Coal" at Rondout, from *Scientific American*, March 2, 1901. Island Dock was an artificial island at the terminus of the D&H Canal.

Courtesy of the Canal Society of New York State

Roebling's Delaware River Aqueduct on the D&H Canal, December, 1923. An auto bridge today, it may be the oldest suspension bridge in the world still in use.

Courtesy of the New York State Library

canal, from Kingston to Honesdale; and a 16-mile-long railroad, from Honesdale to the mines at Carbondale.[117] The 105-mile canal posed no unusual engineering problems, and was considered a routine project. The same could not be said for the railroad.

Building a railroad in the United States in 1827 was out of the ordinary. The only other railroads under way at that time were the Quincy, in Massachusetts, and the Mauch Chunk, in Pennsylvania. Thus, with regard to transportation technology, the railroad portion of the Delaware and Hudson project was perhaps more significant an achievement than the canal, except for the Roebling aqueducts. John B. Jervis was responsible for constructing the railroad. He succeeded Wright as chief engineer in 1827 and became one of the leading civil engineers in nineteenth-century America.

Part of the challenge of designing the railroad was that it had to overcome a 900-foot ascent from Carbondale to the summit level. Jervis decided to use 35-horsepower, high-pressure, stationary steam engines to haul the loaded three-ton coal cars up the steep inclines; gravity would take them down the opposite slopes which, in the process, would pull empty cars back up the inclines. Hence, the name "gravity railroad" was applied. For the more level stretches of the road, Jervis purchased four steam locomotives. This was a novelty, since locomotives were not used on the two other roads under construction.[118] Three of the engines were ordered from the celebrated English builder, Robert Stephenson, in Newcastle. The other of an older colliery design came from Foster, Rastrick and Company, in Stourbridge.

The Stourbridge Lion and Stevenson's America both arrived on the same canal boat and were the only locomotives delivered.[119] A few days later, early in August 1829, the Stourbridge Lion lumbered down the track on its trial run. Unfortunately, the eight-ton Lion exceeded the carrying capacity of the timber-and-iron rails by 50 percent, resulting in the decision not to use locomotive power on the railroad. (Eventually, other locomotives were purchased and put into operation.) Though a failure for its intended purpose, the Stourbridge Lion has been recognized as the first locomotive to run on a track in the United States,[120] though currently there is some debate over whether that distinction should go to the America instead. The vestiges of the Stourbridge Lion—its boiler and one piston—can now be seen at the National Museum of American History of the Smithsonian.

Before the gravity railroad was operational, the canal's appetite for coal was satisfied by wagonloads of the black rock laboriously hauled over the Moosic Mountains to Honesdale. On December 5, 1828, two months after the Delaware and Hudson Canal opened, a flotilla of 11 boats, each carrying ten tons, brought the first Carbondale coal to Rondout, near Kingston. There, coal was heaped in immense piles on an artificial island in Rondout Creek, which empties into the Hudson, for transshipment. The canal utilized the stretch of the Rondout Creek below Eddyville; boats were let into the Creek at Eddyville's tidewater lock.[121]

When opened, the Delaware and Hudson Canal crossed the Delaware River by means of guard locks and slack-water navigation. This situation was never popular with people who made their living rafting logs down the river to Philadelphia. The dam built to achieve slack water in the river and the increased canal traffic interrupted the rafting trade. As a result, company managers authorized construction of two aqueducts in 1846, one over the Delaware and the other across the Lackawaxen a short distance upstream from its junction with the Delaware. John Roebling was hired to build the wire suspension structures, with wooden troughs to hold the canal water. Roebling finished the first two suspension aqueducts in 1848, then built another across the Rondout Creek at High Falls, and one over the Neversink River the following year.[122] The Roebling suspension aqueducts were a novelty at the time, and they were so well constructed that one remains in operation. The Delaware Aqueduct no longer carries canal boats across the river, but now serves as an automobile bridge between New York and Pennsylvania. Located some 18 miles upstream from Port Jervis, it is the property of the National Park Service and may well be the oldest wire suspension bridge in the world still in use.

The Delaware Aqueduct has continued in use for almost a century longer than the canal it was built to serve. Although the Delaware and Hudson Canal's primary purpose—coal transportation—kept its usage high during early years of operation, after the Civil War, railroads began to cut into its trade. By the 1870s, the Delaware and Hudson Canal Company succeeded in gaining control of the Albany and Susquehanna Railroad between New York's capital and Binghamton. With this, canal operations began to wane, and in 1899 the canal was abandoned. A brief rejuvenation came in 1902, when the High Falls-to-Eddyville section was sold to the Consolidated Rosendale Cement Company, which used it to haul cement. Although this vestige of the canal showed a profit for a time, it too faded into history after approximately a decade.[123] Overgrown locks and a few aqueduct abutments remain as mute evidence of New York's most profitable private canal enterprise.

Junction Canal

BOTH NEW YORK AND PENNSYLVANIA built extensive canal systems during the first half of the nineteenth century. The completion of New York's Chemung Canal in 1833 opened a waterway from Elmira, near the Pennsylvania border, to the Erie Canal. Soon after the Chemung was opened, agitation began for a connection between Elmira and Pennsylvania's canals to bring coal into western New York in exchange for limestone and gypsum.[124] About the time that construction might have started on an artificial water link, the Depression of 1837 intervened and plans were scrapped. Then, in 1842, the Pennsylvania Legislature chartered the North Branch Canal Company to complete a canal from Pittston to Athens, near the New York line. This action prompted investors in Elmira to petition the New York Legislature to incorporate the Junction Canal Company to make the connection with the North Branch Canal.[125]

Although construction was put off until early 1853, within a year most of the waterway had been completed. Delays in completing Pennsylvania's portion resulted a state takeover of the project. The connection finally occurred late in 1856, when two boatloads of Pennsylvania anthracite arrived at Elmira. The 18-mile Junction Canal was 40 feet wide and 4 feet deep, allowing for vessels of 75-ton capacity.[126]

In 1858, Pennsylvania sold the North Branch Extension to the North Branch Canal Company. Principals in the Junction Canal Company also owned shares in the North Branch Canal Company; prominent among them was John Arnot, a successful Elmira banker and railroad promoter.[127] The renewed viability of the North Branch caused trade on the Junction to grow. The chief cargo was anthracite, which rose from a total of 32,453 tons in 1858 to 43,147 tons by 1860; bituminous coal also was carried on the canal and amounted to about half the hard-coal tonnage. Toll income similarly increased, from $11,656 to $13,069 by 1860, though it still was relatively small compared to the size of the investment.[128] With the outbreak of the Civil War, shipping continued to increase, and by the middle of the conflict in 1863 toll collection amounted to over $25,000, against operating expenses of less than $10,000.[129]

Just when it appeared that the two companies were headed toward financial success, a devastating flood hit the region in March 1865. The North Branch Extension Canal was almost totally destroyed, and the Junction Canal also suffered considerable damage. Although the canals were repaired and reopened, both companies began to look to railroads as a more profitable alternative. As they pushed track through the area, canal use began to fall.[130] Then, in 1871, floods in the Chemung River reduced coal shipments to Elmira via the Junction to only 511 tons for that year. The end came the following year, when the company tersely reported that the "canal was not opened this year, and will not be."[131] With that came the close of corporate canalling in New York's southern tier.

V. Long Island's Canal

IN 1906, Noble Whitford wrote that when it built "the Shinnecock and Peconic canal. . .New York opened the only salt-water canal" owned by the state, "and also the only one constructed for more than purposes of transportation." Whitford explained that even though "the cost [of the canal] has been large, the renewed fish, clam, and oyster industries are said to much more then [*sic*] compensate all expenditures."[132]

The canal connects two bays on opposite sides of Long Island's south fork, and thus separates Southampton and Easthampton townships from the rest of Suffolk County. Local lore places a narrow channel at that site in pre-colonial times (opened by Native Americans before the arrival of the Europeans). In any case, the legislature approved a survey for the waterway in 1879. In his survey report the following year, State Engineer Horatio Seymour, Jr., referred to an 1826 recommendation by engineer Holmes Hutchinson which gave rise to two companies, the Long Island Canal Company (incorporated in 1828) and the Long Island Canal and Navigation Company (organized in 1848). The purpose of both companies was to build a canal; neither one achieved its goal.[133]

To a large extent, Seymour's report incorporated Hutchinson's plan for the canal. Seymour noted a difference in water elevation between the two bays that at times was as much as two-and-a-half feet. The flow caused by the unequal levels would be up to 330 feet per minute—five times the safe limit for a canal with sand banks. The recommended solution was to construct a lock with a double set of gates to protect the canal banks against the action of the current and to allow passage of boats at any stage of tide.[134]

Although construction started in 1884, work proceeded painfully slowly—incredibly, it took until the end of 1892 to complete the 4,000-foot canal. Instead of the recommended locks, tide gates were installed that would allow water to flow into Shinnecock Bay at high tide but would prevent it from rushing back with harmful force. As constructed, the canal continues in operation today.

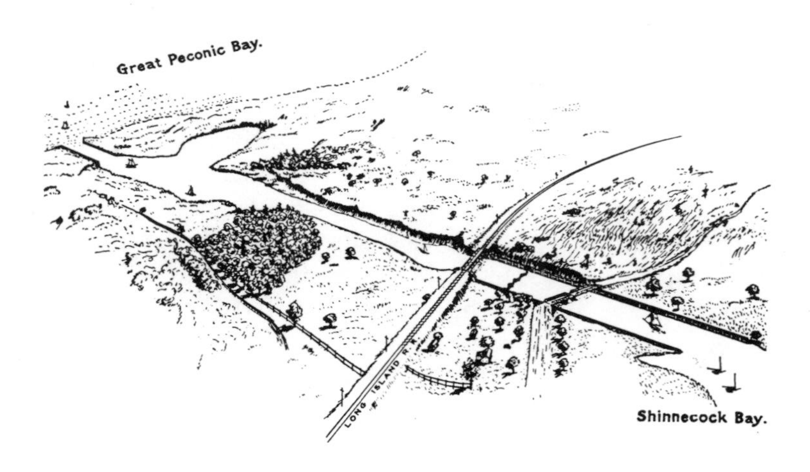

Long Island's Canal.
From Whitford, Vol. 1.

VI. The Barge Canal System

WITH THE TURN OF THE TWENTIETH CENTURY, New York's surviving canals faced new challenges. Under the terms of a measure approved in 1895, the Erie was undergoing its second enlargement with a deepening to nine feet. Bonds totaling $9 million were issued to cover the cost of improvements to the Erie, the Champlain, and the Oswego Canals. Three years later, a gubernatorial report complained that only two-thirds of the work was completed but all the money had been spent.[135] Although an investigative commission blamed the state engineer and the superintendent of public works, evidence indicated that the $9 million was insufficient to complete the envisioned improvements.[136]

Theodore Roosevelt, who became governor in 1899, named a committee to review the entire canal situation. On January 15, 1900, it reported in favor of keeping the state's canals in operation and enlarging the Erie, Champlain, and Oswego Canals. It recommended dredging the Erie to a depth of 12 feet in order to accommodate barges of 1,000 tons.[137]

In 1901, the Erie's traffic still managed to top two million tons, but none of the other four major state canals carried over a million tons; the last-place Oswego moved barely more than 43,000, and the total tonnage for the Black River was only 68,500.[138] Clearly, revitalization was needed. A majority of the state legislature agreed, and in 1903 another enlargement and other changes were approved as part of the *Barge Canal Act*.[139] The Erie, Champlain, Oswego, and Cayuga and Seneca canals were amalgamated into the New York State Barge Canal System. These four canals, together with the Hudson River and the several lakes connected with the canals, gave the new system a total length of more than 800 miles.[140] (Exclusion from the Barge Canal doomed the Black River Canal to extinction.)

The Barge Canal System utilizes a number of rivers and lakes in addition to its constructed segments. Between Waterford and Rome, the Barge Canal is mainly the Mohawk River; from Rome to Rochester, it passes through Oneida Lake and the Oneida, Seneca, and Clyde Rivers; west of Rochester it is a constructed channel until it reaches Lockport, then for the rest of the way the Tonawanda Creek is used. The lower portion of the Champlain is the Hudson River, and both the Oswego and the Seneca and Cayuga are mainly controlled rivers.

The artificial channel width of the Barge Canal is 200 or more feet in the natural waterways, 75 feet in earth, and 94 feet in rock, all with a minimum depth of 12 feet. The canal's 57 main-line concrete locks measure 44.5 by 300 feet, with lifts ranging between 6 feet and 40.5 feet. Steel lock gates, some of which weigh over 200 tons, are electrically operated, as are the water-control valves. The 169-foot combined lift of Waterford's five locks is "twice as much as the total lift from sea-level to summit of the Panama Canal," and the 40.5-foot lift of the Little Falls lock is greater than any Panama Canal lock.[141]

An unusual feature found at some locks are the power houses. These contained the turbines and other machinery that generated power from the flow of water through special tunnels from a higher to a lower level in the lock. The

Construction of Erie Barge Canal Lock 5, Waterford, August 1908.

Cutting the new channel through a loop in the Oneida River for the Erie Barge Canal, May 1908.

Both courtesy of the New York State Archives

electricity was used to operate one or more locks, and on some occasions even was transmitted over short distances.[142] But gasoline-powered machinery was used to raise and lower the canal's moveable dams that were built in the Mohawk River to maintain the required water level since draining the canal in winter prevented the generation of electricity. Eventhough no longer used for their intended purpose, some power houses still stand near canal locks, and they contain the original turbines and shiny brass and copper fixtures used to generate electricity.[143]

Sources of water to maintain a constant canal depth was less a problem for the Barge Canal west of Rome than east of that city. To guarantee the needed supply, the upper Mohawk River and one of its feeders, the West Canada Creek, were dammed to form two reservoirs. Both the resultant Delta Lake (north of Rome) and Hinkley Lake (north of Herkimer) are slightly over four square miles in area and provide an ample supply of water for the canal. Water depth in the Mohawk between Rome and Waterford is maintained by control dams, most of which have movable gates and steel superstructures that resemble highway bridges. During winters and floods, the hinged gates are swung up under the "bridge" section, allowing the natural flow of this river.[144]

The entire Barge Canal System was operational by 1918 and cost $155 million. In addition to pleasure boats and old Erie Canal barges pulled by tug boats, several types of new commercial craft appeared on the waterway. One early experiment in the latter part of World War I saw barges made of concrete, a substitute for steel, which was needed for the war effort. Contracts were let for 25 concrete vessels, with sides of four-inch-thick reinforced concrete, costing $25,000 each. These floating cement vaults were unsuccessful due to their excessive draw (four feet when empty, compared to the maximum of 22 inches of a wood or steel barge) and the ease with which the sides were holed (and the barges sunk) when they struck a solid object.[145] With a useful life of not more than four years, some of the concrete barges eventually were used to fill in the old Erie Canal at Buffalo, and others still can be seen during the winter when the water is low, near lock nine.[146]

Another kind of barge was 150 feet long by 20 feet wide, with a 650-ton cargo capacity. These operated in fleets of four, with a self-propelled lead barge towing the other three. The motorized barge had a capacity of only 350 tons due to the placement of the engine. Another type was 100 feet long by 20.5 feet wide, with a capacity of 400 to 500 tons; these were pulled by tugs in fleets of five. A third variety was a 250-foot by 30-foot steel motorship with a 1,600-ton capacity.[147]

Henry Ford constructed four huge motorships in the 1930s specifically for Barge Canal transportation. Measuring 290 feet long, each one could swallow 2,800 to 3,000 tons of almost any canal cargo. These monsters were powered by twin diesel engines, each producing 600 to 800 horsepower. Ford's vessels plied the canal until the entry of the United States into World War II, when they were drafted for duty in the Caribbean. One of the Ford ships, the *Green Island*, was a war casualty. In January 1942, it suffered some damage when mistakenly rammed by the destroyer U.S.S. *Hamilton*. The ill-fated *Green Island* met final destruction later that year when it was sunk by the German *U-125* off Jamaica. Fortunately, the submarine commandeer allowed the crew to take to the lifeboats before he torpedoed the craft.[148]

Ford was not the only company to use the Barge Canal. General Electric shipped finished products to New York City and raw materials made the return trip to the company's plant in Schenectady. SOCONY, starting with just a tug and a barge, moved 14,000 tons of oil in 1918 alone to cities between Schenectady and Rome on the Erie, and to Fort Edward and Whitehall on the Champlain section. The 22 barges of the Ore Carrying Company of New York City brought iron ore from Port Henry on Lake Champlain and returned laden with coal. The oldest and largest business using the canal was the Lake Champlain Transportation Company, operating out of Whitehall. The Sugar Producing Company, with its four tank barges, moved large quantities of molasses at less than half the cost of rail shipment. Other companies used the Barge Canal as well, taking advantage of its low bulk-cargo rates.

But, apparently not enough firms favored water transportation.[149] Between 1918 and 1924, the system's traffic averaged 169,000 tons per year. Even the increase to 1,238,844 tons (in 1925) did not approach the Barge Canal's estimated annual capacity of 10 million tons.[150] A report published the following year claimed it would be cheaper to pay for canal

The canal motorship *Day Peckinpaugh* on its last voyage on the Barge Canal after 70 years in service, Phoenix, Sept. 6, 1994.

Courtesy of the Canal Society of New York State

freight to be carried on railroads than to maintain the canal. Reduced usage was blamed on the long winter closings and the low bridge clearances, yet it was noted that the St. Lawrence ship canals were successful, even though they were closed in winter, and the Welland Canal was continually improved to help keep its income up.[151]

Traffic did rise throughout the late 1920s and, after falling again during the Depression, rebounded during World War II and peaked in the mid-1950s. But the opening of the St. Lawrence Seaway, which could accommodate ocean-going vessels, took its toll on the Barge Canal after 1959. Within a quarter century, commercial shipments on the Barge dwindled to almost none.[152] The sad situation becomes much more vivid when commodities are viewed from a "last year shipped" perspective: The Barge Canal last carried flour in 1950, brick in 1954, iron ore in 1955, and oats in 1959; coal has not been seen on the canal since 1962, lumber since 1963, wheat since 1968, paper since 1972, and sugar since 1976.[153] During the two years prior to 1991, no freight at all was handled at 49 of the canal's 66 terminals, and only five of its 53 warehouses were used for their intended purpose.[154] In June 1995, when this author spent three delightful and scenic days on the canal steaming from Syracuse to Buffalo, the only other commercial traffic seen were two or three dinner boats.

The number of pleasure boats passing through at least one lock averaged approximately 131,000 for the decade after 1982. Slightly more than half of the private craft sailed on the Erie section, with boat numbers on the Champlain, Oswego, and Cayuga and Seneca sections following in order.[155] In 1992, the New York State Legislature transferred responsibility for the canals from the Department of Transportation to the Thruway Authority, established a Canal Recreationway Commission to work with the Thruway Authority to chart the future of the canals, and renamed the Barge Canal the New York State Canal System.

VII. The St. Lawrence Seaway

THE FIVE GREAT LAKES span the distance from New York to Minnesota along the northern boundary of the United States. The single outlet of these inland seas is the mighty St. Lawrence River, which flows from the northeast corner of Lake Ontario to its meeting with the Atlantic at the Gulf of St. Lawrence.

In 1535, French explorers were the first recorded Europeans to push upstream in the great river. Led by Jacques Cartier, they gave the river its present name and coursed westerly as far as the future location of Montreal. Their ships could not pass beyond that point because of the enormous rapids extending 100 miles upstream. The French called the first stretch of raging water La Chine (surely, they thought, the great river must lead through the continental land mass to the Pacific and China). In time, other French voyageurs and fur traders paddled smaller craft upstream past La Chine and other rapids they named Cascades, Cedar, Coteau, and the longest, Long Sault. Canoes could pass the rapids, but if trade in any volume was to occur, the treacherous flumes would have to be bypassed.

After 1763, when the British wrested Canada from the French, a series of narrow canals with lift locks were built to circumvent the rapids. Water depth in the locks was only two-and-a-half feet, but it was sufficient to float the flat-bottomed bateaux that plied the river. The bateaux were at times propelled by sail, but they mostly depended on the endurance of four to eight hardy voyageurs. It took nearly a week to make the 175-mile passage from Montreal to Kingston, Ontario, at the head of the St. Lawrence.[156] The capacity of bateaux was greater than that of canoes, but still fell short of what was needed for the growing trade.

The first ship canal opened along the route of the future "seaway" to Lake Superior was not built along the St. Lawrence, but resulted from the need to avoid Niagara Falls, where Lake Erie empties into Lake Ontario. The Welland Canal, opened in 1833, paralleled the Niagara River in Canada. It connected Lake Erie with Lake Ontario and accommodated ships up to 125 tons pulled by horses that walked a towpath. Although a goal of the Welland Canal was to take trade away from the mighty Erie Canal, to an extent it instead supplemented New York's waterway—shippers often used the Welland as an alternate route from Lake Erie to New York City via the Oswego and Erie Canals. Although it involved the added expense of moving cargo from the larger lake boats to the smaller canal craft, it was a more direct route to the Atlantic and it avoided the wild downstream ride through the St. Lawrence rapids. So, if Canada hoped to challenge New York's hold on the western trade, a ship canal around the rapids was a must.

By 1848, against seemingly endless difficulties—including the powerful river current, rocky soil, influence peddling, and labor problems—a St. Lawrence waterway was completed with a series of locks and short canals and a water depth of nine feet. Although the trip from Lake Erie to Montreal on the waterway took only a quarter of the time it took to get from Lake Erie to New York City, Montreal still did not supplant the ice-free New York port as North America's principal *entrepôt* with Europe.[157]

But the completion of the St. Lawrence ship canals offered an unanticipated opportunity for a tourist attraction. Small steamers loaded with thrill seekers left upper river ports to run downstream through the immense rapids to Montreal; they used the canals for the return trip. That "sport" started around 1850 and lasted for the next century. At its height in the early twentieth century, more than 100,000 passengers experienced the excitement each year. By then the ships that ran the rapids had double-steel hulls as insurance against being crushed by boulders in the river. Still, there were accidents, often initiated by steering gear breaks, which caused ships to plunge through the maelstrom out of control, resulting in grounding. Amazingly, there was little loss of life.[158] Seaway construction in the 1950s and the resultant flooding of the breathtaking St. Lawrence rapids brought an end to the thrilling activity.

In 1895, the United States and Canada jointly appointed a Deep Waterways Commission to recommend navigation routes between the Atlantic Ocean and the Great Lakes—the first cooperative international board to study the possibility of a seaway. This initial effort was extended by the Boundary Waters Treaty of 1909, which defined the rights of both nations regarding navigation of boundary waters and also created an International Joint Commission to further regulate use of common waters. Twelve years later, the International Joint Commission recommended Canada and the

Facing Page:

Official opening of the Saint Lawrence Seaway with Governor Rockefeller, Queen Elizabeth, and Vice President Nixon, June 1959.

Courtesy of the New York State Archives

United States jointly improve the St. Lawrence from Lake Ontario to Montreal. This cooperation led to the signing of the St. Lawrence Treaty in 1932, in which both nations agreed to equally share construction costs of a waterway from the Atlantic all the way to Lake Superior. Any electric power generated by the project also would be equally shared. The United States Senate failed to ratify the treaty.[159]

The outbreak of World War II brought about renewed interest in the project, and a new treaty was written in 1941. This second attempt met the same fate in the Senate as the earlier effort, as did a 1947 proposal. The latter provided for the collection of tolls to pay the cost of construction; the delay was due largely to opposition from states on the East and Gulf Coasts.[160] The breakdown of negotiations caused New York and Ontario to open talks for the development of St. Lawrence power. Finally, in 1954, the United States agreed to joint development, with both nations participating in the construction of a seaway in the international section of the St. Lawrence. Support from President Eisenhower and American steel companies facilitated the agreement. Depletion of the legendary Mesabi Range on Lake Superior, coupled with new discoveries of iron ore in Labrador, spurred the steel companies' support, since a St. Lawrence seaway could get Labrador ore to the U. S. mills in the Great Lakes region.[161]

The necessity for a minimum 27-foot navigation depth and the 860-foot-long locks for the seaway helped drive the costs for the Montreal-to-Lake Ontario section to $124 million for the United States and $285 million for Canada.[162] A major portion of the $409 million went for actual construction, but some of the money was needed for the relocation of villages along the route. By July 1958, the project was largely completed.

The St. Lawrence Seaway has had an impact on many border states as well as on Canada. Its commercial effect on

New York centered on the Ogdensburg vicinity, where Reynolds Aluminum and General Motors both have built plants. Of course, the New York ports of Oswego, Rochester, and Buffalo also have felt the seaway's impact. Another of the seaway's effects on New York (and the reason for Reynolds Aluminum's location) was the available electric power.

The seaway's power dams serve New York, New England, and parts of Canada, and produce an estimated 3.5 million kilowatts of electricity; the Moses-Saunders Dam between New York State and Ontario is one of the largest power-producing dams in the world, with a 1.9-million kilowatt capability. In addition to heavy industrial consumption, St. Lawrence electricity eventually became available to more than 600,000 residential consumers in places as far south as Albany and Oswego.[163]

Today, tourists enjoying the picturesque St. Lawrence are often startled to see the great steel sides of ocean vessels slide by. With the completion of the St. Lawrence Seaway, New York's canal experience has come full circle. It began two centuries ago as an improved natural waterway system, and it has returned to the same, today.

Overleaf:

The gravestone of canal contractor Luke Hitchcock (1789-1860), now on the grounds of the Madison County Historical Society.

Courtesy of the New York State Museum

LUKE HITCHCOCK,
BORN
NOV. 14TH, 1789,
DIED
MAY 1ST, 1860.

Notes

[1]"Robert Livingston's Report of a Journey to Onondaga," in E. B. O'Callaghan, ed., *Documents Relative to the Colonial History of the State of New York* (Albany: Weed, Parsons and Co., 1853-87), IV, p.650.

[2]"Conference of Lord Cornbury with the Indians," in O'Callaghan, ibid., p.979.

[3]Ibid., p.981.

[4]Daniel Wager, *Oneida County*, New York (Boston: Boston History Co., 1896), p.4.

[5]Robert E. Hager, *Mohawk River Boats and Navigation before 1820* (Syracuse: Canal Society of New York State, 1987), p.22.

[6]Ronald E. Shaw, *Erie Water West* (Lexington: University of Kentucky Press, 1966), p.19.

[7]Ibid., p.18.

[8]Ibid., pp.45-46.

[9]Noble E. Whitford, *History of the Canal System of the State of New York* (Albany: Brandow Printing, 1906), I, pp.90-91.

[10]Ibid., p.88.

[11]Ibid., pp.96-97.

[12]Carol Sheriff, *The Artificial River: The Erie Canal and the Paradox of Progress, 1817-1862*,(New York: Hill and Wang, 1996), pp.40-41.

[13]Shaw, *Erie Water West*, pp.125-128.

[14]Ibid., pp.130-131.

[15]Ibid., pp.134-135.

[16]Whitford, I, pp.124-126.

[17]Ibid., pp.127-129.

[18]Walter D. Edmonds, *Rome Haul* (Syracuse: Syracuse University Press, 1987), p.8.

[19]Shaw, *Erie Water West*, pp.197-206.

[20]Ibid., p.208.

[21]Ibid., p.209.

[22]Ibid.

[23]Sheriff, 53.

[24]Ibid.

[25]Robert G. Albion, *The Rise of New York Port, 1815-1860* (Boston: Northeastern University Press; and New York: South Street Seaport Museum, 1984), p.88.

[26]Whitney R. Cross, *The Burned-Over District* (Ithaca: Cornell University Press, 1950), p.56.

[27]Whitford, I, p.914.

[28]Ulysses P. Hedrick, *A History of Agriculture in the State of New York* (New York: Hill & Wang, 1966), p.247.

[29]Albion, p.88.

[30]Whitford, I, p.914.

[31]Albion, p.91.

[32]Whitford, I, p.910.

[33]Cross, p.56.

[34]Hedrick, p.247.

[35]Cross, p.59.

[36]Hedrick, p.248.

[37]Albion, p.77.

[38]Ibid., p.92.

[39]Ibid., p.94.

[40]Shaw, *Erie Water West*, p.241.

[41]Whitford, II, p.1030.

[42]Ibid., II, pp.1062-1063.

[43]Ibid., I, p.910.

[44]F. Daniel Larkin, *Pioneer American Railroads: The Mohawk and Hudson & the Saratoga and Schenectady* (Fleischmanns, NY: Purple Mountain Press, 1995), pp.21-22.

[45]Ibid., p.39.

[46]Ibid., p.62.

[47]Whitford, I, p.911.

[48]Ibid., II, p.1030.

[49]Ibid., I, p.410.

[50]Ibid., I, p.411.

[51]Ibid., II, p.1031.

[52]Horatio Gates Spafford, *Gazetteer of the State of New-York*, (Albany: D. B. Packard, 1824; rpt. Interlaken, NY: Heart of the Lakes Publishing, 1981), pp.96-97.

[53]Ibid., p.98.

[54]Hedrick, p.246.

[55]Whitford, II, pp.1062-1065.

[56]Ronald Shaw, *Canals for a Nation* (Lexington: The University of Kentucky Press, 1990), p.56.

[57]"Castorland Journal," unpublished copy of the original made by the Remsen-Steuben Historical Society, Remsen, NY, 1980, p.77.

[58]Whitford, I, pp.448-449.

[59]Ibid., pp.451-452.

[60]Ibid., II, p.1031.

[61]J. H. French, *Gazetteer of the State of New York* (Syracuse: R. P. Smith, 1860; rpt. Interlaken, NY: Heart of the Lakes Publishing, 1980), p.56.

[62]Whitford, II, p.1032.

[63]Ibid., II, pp.1062-1065.

[64]Ibid., I, pp.472-473.

[65]Ibid., II, p.1032.

[66]Ibid.

[67]Ibid.

[68]Ibid., I, pp.607-608.

[69]Ibid., I, pp.611-612.

[70]Ibid., II, p.1033.

[71]Ibid., I, p.617.

[72]Ibid.

[73]Ibid., II, p.1062.

[74]Ibid., I, pp.624-626.

[75]Ibid., II, pp.1062-1063.

[76]*New York State Constitution, Annotated* (New York State Constitutional Convention Commission, 1938), Vol. I, part II, pp.65, 91.

[77]Whitford, I, pp.640-642.

[78]Ibid., I, pp.644-654.

[79]Ibid., II, pp.1064-1065.

[80]Ibid.

[81]Ibid., I, pp.651-652.

[82]Ibid., I, pp.657-658.

[83]Ibid., I, pp.658-659.

[84]Ibid., I, pp.660-662.

[85]Ibid., I, pp.669-670.

[86]F. Daniel Larkin, *John B. Jervis, An American Engineering Pioneer* (Ames: Iowa State University Press, 1990), pp.52-53.

[87]Ibid., pp.53-55.

[88]Michele A. McFee, *Limestone Locks and Overgrowth* (Fleischmanns, NY: Purple Mountain Press, 1993), pp.57-58.

[89]Ibid., p.57.

[90]Ibid.

[91]Whitford, II, p.1034.

[92]McFee, p.125.

[93]Ibid., pp.170-171.

[94]Ibid., p.107.

[95]Ibid., p. 190-199.

[96]Whitford, II, p.1063.

[97]Ibid., I, pp.708-709.

[98]Ibid., II, p.1035.

[99]Gladys Reid Holton, "The Genesee Valley Canal," unpublished manuscript in the New York State Library, Albany, NY, 1958, pp.6-7.

[100]Ibid.

[101]Whitford, II, p.1035.

[102]Holton, p.10.

[103]Whitford, II, pp.1062-1063.

[104]Holton, p.10.

[105]Shaw, *Canals for a Nation*, p.45.

[106]F. Daniel Larkin, "The Black River Canal: A Waterway to the North Country," *The Hudson Valley Regional Review*, March 1993, p.6.

[107]Ibid., p.8.

[108]Ibid., pp.8-9.

[109]Ibid., pp.10-11.

[110]Ibid., p.12.

[111]Ibid., pp.12-13.

[112]Ibid., pp.15-16.

[113]Ibid., pp.19-20.

[114]Ibid., p.20.

[115]Ibid., p.21.

[116]Manville B. Wakefield, *Coal Boats to Tidewater* (Fleischmanns, NY: Purple Mountain Press, 1992), pp.3-4.

[117]Larkin, *John B. Jervis*, pp.18-19.

[118]Ibid., pp.25-28.

[119]John B. Jervis to John Bolton, Honesdale, Pa., August 1, 1829, Jervis MSS, Jervis Public Library, Rome, NY.

[120]Ibid.

[121]Wakefield, p.7.

[122]Ibid., pp.83-89.

[123]Larry Lowenthal, *From the Coal Fields to the Hudson* (Fleischmanns, NY: Purple Mountain Press, 1997), pp.275-276.

[124]Charles Petrillo, "The Junction Canal (1855-1871): Elmira, New York, to Athens, PA," *Canal History and Technology Proceedings*, Vol. X (Easton, PA: Center for Canal History and Technology, 1991), p.184.

[125]Terry K. Woods, "The Junction Canal," *The Best from American Canals*, No. III (York, Pennsylvania: The American Canal and Transportation Center, 1986), pp.30-31.

[126]Ibid., pp.30-31.

[127]Petrillo, pp.186-187.

[128]Ibid., p.199.

[129]Woods, p.31.

[130]Petrillo, pp.201-205.

[131]Woods, p.31.

[132]Whitford, I, p.576.

[133]Ibid., pp.577-578.

[134]Ibid., I, p.578.

[135]Ibid., 355-56.

[136]Ibid., 373-75.

[137]Ibid., 382-83.

[138]Ibid., II, p.1063.

[139]Ibid., p. 393-95.

[140]Roy G. Finch, State Engineer and Surveyor, *The Story of New York State Canals* (Albany: J. B. Lyon, 1925), pp.9-11.

[141]Ibid., pp.12-15.

[142]Noble E. Whitford, *History of the Barge Canal of New York State* (Albany, N.Y.: J. B. Lyon Co., 1922), p. 494.

[143]Ibid.

[144]Ibid., p.495.

[145]Finch, p. 13.

[146]Richard Garrity, *Canal Boatman* (Syracuse: Syracuse University Press, 1977), pp.179-180.

[177]Ibid., p.17.

[148]Bill Ortell, "Ford's Barge Canal Fleet," *Bottoming Out* (Syracuse: Canal Society of New York State, 1996), pp.16-23.

[149]Charles T. O'Malley, *Low Bridges and High Water on the New York State Barge Canal* (Ellenton, FL: Diamond Mohawk Publishing, 1991), p.35.

[150]Ibid., p.36.

[151]Ibid., p.37.

[152]Ibid., p.278.

[153]Ibid., p.277.

[154]Ibid., p.38.

[155]*New York State Statistical Yearbook*, 1994 (Albany: The Nelson A. Rockefeller Institute of Government, 1994), p.465.

[156]Carleton Mabee, *The Seaway Story* (New York: Macmillan, 1961), pp.9-10.

[157]Ibid., pp.22-25.

[158]Ibid., pp.36-40.

[159]Gennifer Sussman, *The St. Lawrence Seaway: History and Analysis of a Joint Water Highway* (Montreal: C. D. Howe Research Institute; and Washington, D. C.: National Planning Association, 1978), pp.18-20.

[160]Mabee, p.145.

[161]Ibid., pp.145-149.

[162]Sussman, pp.23-24.

[163]Mabee, pp.223-237.

References

Albion, Robert G. *The Rise of New York Port, 1815-1860*. Boston: Northeastern University Press; and New York: South Street Seaport Museum, 1984.

"Castorland Journal." Unpublished manuscript. Remsen-Steuben Historical Society, Remsen, NY, 1980.

Cross, Whitney R. *The Burned Over District: The Social and Intellectual History of Enthusiastic Religion in Western New York, 1800-1850*. Ithaca: Cornell University Press, 1950; rpt. New York: Octagon Books, 1981.

Edmonds, Walter D. *Rome Haul*. Syracuse: Syracuse University Press, 1987.

Finch, Roy G. *The Story of New York State Canals: Historical and Commercial Information*. Albany: J. B. Lyon, 1925.

French, J. H. *Gazetteer of the State of New York*. Syracuse: R. P. Smith, 1860; rpt. Interlaken, NY: Heart of the Lakes Publishing, 1980.

Garrity, Richard. *Canal Boatman*. Syracuse: Syracuse University Press, 1977.

Hager, Robert E. *Mohawk River Boats and Navigation Before 1820*. Syracuse: Canal Society of New York State, 1987.

Hedrick, Ulysses P. *A History of Agriculture in the State of New York*. New York: Hill and Wang, 1966.

Holton, Gladys Reid. "The Genesee Valley Canal." Unpublished manuscript. New York State Library, Albany, NY, 1958.

John Jervis MSS. Jervis Public Library, Rome, NY.

Larkin, F. Daniel. *John B. Jervis: An American Engineering Pioneer*. Ames: Iowa State University Press, 1990.

___. *Pioneer American Railroads: The Mohawk and Hudson & the Saratoga and Schenectady*. Fleischmanns, NY: Purple Mountain Press, 1995.

___. "The Black River Canal: A Waterway to the North Country." *The Hudson Valley Regional Review*, March 1993.

Lowenthal, Larry. *From the Coal Fields to the Hudson: A History of the Delaware & Hudson Canal*. Fleischmanns, NY: Purple Mountain Press, 1997.

McFee, Michele A. *Limestone Locks and Overgrowth: The Rise and Descent of the Chenango Canal*. Fleischmanns, NY: Purple Mountain Press, 1993.

Mabee, Carleton. *The Seaway Story*. New York: Macmillan Co., 1961.

New York State Constitution, Annotated. Albany: New York State Constitutional Convention Commission, 1938.

New York State Statistical Yearbook, 1994. Albany: The Nelson A. Rockefeller Institute of Government, 1994.

O'Callaghan, E[mund] B[ailey], ed. *Documents Relative to the Colonial History of the State of New York.* 15 vols. Albany: Weed, Parsons and Co., 1853-1887.

O'Malley, Charles T. *Low Bridges and High Water on the New York State Barge Canal.* Ellenton, FL: Diamond Mohawk Publishing, 1991.

Ortell, Bill. "Ford's Barge Canal Fleet." *Bottoming Out.* Syracuse: Canal Society of New York State, 1996.

Petrillo, Charles. "The Junction Canal (1855-1871): Elmira, New York, to Athens, Pennsylvania." *Canal History and Technology Proceedings*, Vol. X. Easton, PA: Center for Canal History and Technology, 1991.

Shaw, Ronald. *Canals for a Nation: The Canal Era in the United States, 1790-1860.* Lexington: University of Kentucky Press, 1990.

___. *Erie Water West: A History of the Erie Canal, 1792-1854.* Lexington: University of Kentucky Press, 1966; rpt. 1990.

Sheriff, Carol. *The Artificial River: The Erie Canal and the Paradox of Progress, 1817-1862.* New York: Hill & Wang, 1996.

Spafford, Horatio Gates. *Gazetteer of the State of New-York.* Albany: B. D. Packard, 1824; rpt. Interlaken, NY: Heart of the Lakes Publishing, 1981.

Sussman, Gennifer. *The St. Lawrence Seaway: History and Analysis of a Joint Water Highway.* Montreal: C. D. Howe Research Institute and Washington, D. C.: National Planning Association, 1978.

Wager, Daniel. *Oneida County, New York.* Boston: Boston History Company, 1896.

Wakefield, Manville B. *Coal Boats to Tidewater: The Story of the Delaware and Hudson Canal.* Fleischmanns, NY: Purple Mountain Press, 1992.

Whitford, Noble Earl. *History of the Barge Canal of New York State.* Albany, N.Y.: J. B. Lyon Company, 1922.

___. *History of the Canal System of the State of New York, Together with Brief Histories of the Canals of the United States and Canada. . . .* Albany: Brandow Printing Co., 1906.

Woods, Terry K. "The Junction Canal," in *The Best From American Canals, No. III. York, PA: The American Canal and Transportation Center, 1986.*

Index

Acknowledgment

Recognition is due to Craig Williams of the New York State Museum for his thoughtful and valued assistance in the preparation of this book.

About the Author

F. Daniel Larkin, a native of Rome, N.Y., has a PhD in United States History. Currently, he is Interim Provost and Vice President of Academic Affairs at the State University of New York at Oneonta and also holds the academic rank of SUNY Distinguished Service Professor. Dr. Larkin has written extensively, particularly on the topics of the history of technology and New York State history. He is senior author of *New York Yesterday and Today*, and has authored *John B. Jervis: An American Engineering Pioneer* and *Pioneer American Railroads: The Mohawk & Hudson and the Saratoga & Schenectady*, as well as numerous articles on civil engineering, transportation history, and other topics.

About the Publisher

Purple Mountain Press is a publishing company committed to producing the best original books of New York State regional interest as well as bringing back into print significant older works. For a free catalog, write: P.O. Box 309, Fleischmanns, NY 12430, call: 845-254-4062, fax: 845-254-4476, or e-mail: purple@catskill.net.